PRAISE FOR

WHEN LIFE HANDS YOU LEMONS, THROW TOMATOES

"Beautiful in its words, lessons, and recipes, this wonderful book takes you on a journey of family, food, and life. You will relish every page and every dish!"

—**CHESTER ELTON**, author of the *New York Times* bestseller *The Carrot Principle*

When Life Hands You Lemons, Throw Tomatoes offers a harmonious blend of innovative recipes and transformative leadership advice, giving readers a feast for both the mind and the palate. Each chapter serves up delicious dishes paired seamlessly with stories that provide invaluable insights into becoming a more effective, compassionate, and dynamic leader, with a side of humor. This must-read book is more than just a cookbook—it's a manual for living a life of resilience, passion, and purpose."

—**LERZAN AKSOY, PHD**, dean and George N. Jean PhD chair, Gabelli School of Business, Fordham University

"This book is a love letter to the art of cooking, a testament to the power of nostalgia, and a source of inspiration for anyone seeking comfort, connection, and a deeper understanding of life's simple pleasures. Donna invites us into her family's kitchen, not just sharing recipes but cherished family stories and traditions that have been passed down through generations. She is an incredibly accomplished leader and product of deep family roots and strong values."

—**MANDELL CRAWLEY**, chief human resources officer, Morgan Stanley

"I met Donna Rapaccioli about seven years ago, during an event on the campus of Fordham University's Gabelli School of Business. I was very proud of her career as the dean of this impressive business school. As a chef and restauranteur, I realized early in my career that if my passion for cooking was to grow and flourish, I needed to be a good businesswoman, knowing how to balance numbers as well as balance flavors in a sauté pan. It seems that Donna has a gift for both. In her new cookbook, *When Life Hands You Lemons, Throw Tomatoes*, she ventures into the history of her Italian-American family while offering over one hundred recipes that kept that family happy and fed. I found the book utterly charming, with recipes ranging from true Italian to Italian American to personal renditions, along with some of the different ethnic neighborhood flavors thrown in. A fun read with some great recipes to bring it all to the table!"

—**LIDIA BASTIANICH**, Emmy award-winning television host, bestselling cookbook author, and restaurateur

"Most business advice books follow predictably boring formulas. Donna Rapaccioli has instead done something uniquely charming, mixing together a pinch of memoir, a tablespoon of life management advice, a dash of accounting history, and some fabulous recipes that you'll surely enjoy!"

—**CHRIS LOWNEY**, bestselling author of *Heroic Leadership* and *Make Today Matter*

"This book is—almost literally—one to sink your teeth into. Beyond the scrumptious recipes to fill your belly, Donna takes the reader page by page through a journey of food, brilliantly weaving in life and leadership lessons."

—**PATRICIA DAVID**, former chief diversity officer at JP Morgan Chase and author of *The 'Her'story of Davidisms: My Straight-Shooting Answers to 30 Years of Career Questions People Have Asked Me*

WHEN LIFE HANDS YOU LEMONS,

Throw Tomatoes

BE PERSISTENT • TAKE SOME RISK

EMBRACE CHANGE • BE AUTHENTI

BE GENEROUS • LEAD BY EXAMPL

QUALITY MATTERS • COMMUNICAT

MAINTAIN YOUR SENSE OF HUMO

SHOW GRATITUDE • BE CURIOU

BE POSITIVE • SHARE YOUR VISIO

INSPIRE • APPRECIATION MATTER

RESEARCH YOUR OBJECTIV

COLLABORATE • ESTABLISH A VISIO

PROBLEM SOLVE • LISTEN TO LEAR

TEAMS ACHIEVE MORE • SET GOAL

BE CALM • INNOVATE • BE CURIOU

MAKE DECISIONS • SHOW KINDNES

CULTIVATE A SENSE OF BELONGIN

WHEN LIFE HANDS YOU LEMONS,

Throw Tomatoes

LESSONS IN LIFE AND LEADERSHIP

FROM THE KITCHEN OF

Donna Rapaccioli

NQP

NORTH QUARTER PUBLISHERS

Published 2023
Printed in the United States of America
Hardcover ISBN: 979-8-9887504-0-6
Paperback ISBN: 979-8-9887504-1-3
E-ISBN: 979-8-9887504-2-0
Library of Congress Control Number: 2023916476

For information about bulk orders, address:
North Quarter Publishers
Westhampton, NY
info@northquarterpublishers.com

Book design by Stacey Aaronson

Please feel free to alter the recipes contained in this book to your liking. The publisher is not responsible for any adverse reactions to recipes. Please be careful with knives, don't cook recipes with ingredients you are allergic to, and use your best judgment around the kitchen, especially with raw or undercooked ingredients.

This book is dedicated to my husband, Jim, who, since I was a teenager, has been making me feel special and reframing the obstacles we face into new opportunities. The best is yet to come.

CONTENTS

CHAPTER EIGHT: Try It, It's Chicken . . . 109

CHAPTER NINE: Emmy's Cucina . . . 125

EPILOGUE: Compliments of the Chef, Holiday Recipes . . . 141

Cooking More Than the Books

1 am a Bronx girl through and through. My family moved among a few different homes and set up shop in a few different neighborhoods, but never outside the Bronx. We lived in a three-family home that housed multiple generations: my mom and dad, my older brother, and I had the top floor; my maternal grandparents were on the second floor; and my mom's brother and my aunt lived on the first floor. We often ate together (my grandma really knew how to cook), laughed together, and bickered together. No matter what we were up to, we were loud and fun-loving.

When I was eight years old, we all moved to different houses. Mine was just across the street, but my grandparents moved to a new neighborhood. It was only 10 minutes away by car, but to a kid my age, it may as well have been 10 hours. Lucky for me, my grandma—whom my kids would one day call Grandma Millie—let me visit whenever I wanted. Throughout high school and college, I would go to her house to study. Her house was quiet; mine was not. My brother, who was 12 years younger than me, made mine a little too disruptive. Grandma Millie's house was always a peaceful and perfect retreat.

While I hit the books, my grandma pampered me. She cooked me breakfast, lunch, and dinner. Even Quaker packaged oatmeal tasted better when she made it, I'm guessing because of all the butter and salt she added. She was an incredible cook; no matter what she prepared, it was delicious. I still dream about her eggplant rollatini and her Sunday gravy! (You'll get my versions, based largely on hers, on pages 188 and 60.)

Once I got married, I lived right around the block from Grandma Millie. I was a PhD student at NYU then, spending an inordinate amount of time at the table reading and studying. Most mornings, my grandma would go to the grocery store—all her ingredients needed to be fresh—and I could almost always hear her heading back down the block with her squeaky shopping cart. She usually stopped by and came in for a visit. I remember those days like they were yesterday.

I learned from both my mom and grandma the beauty of full-meal cooking, as in, "Let's put out appetizers and make some drinks and enjoy them before we get anywhere near the main course." And, if you thought you were just going to eat a main course and that was that? Nope, you weren't going anywhere, because there was always dessert. On a weeknight!

I'm not usually *that* good, but I've always had a very busy life, whether studying, teaching, consulting, or being the dean of a growing business school, all while trying to balance family. For the most part, I've relegated my homemade full-course meals to the weekends.

Despite these beautiful, shining examples of loving and skilled home cooks in my family, I was a slow starter when it came to cooking for myself. Maybe I wasn't interested in cooking because they did it so well?

But then . . . I got married. It was made very clear to me by my grandmother and mother that it was my responsibility to cook for my husband. He was one of five children, and his mother was also a great cook. So, marching orders in hand, I began my cooking journey. Pretty quickly, I saw the satisfaction my meals brought to my husband and others, and I began investing more time in learning the art and science of cooking.

My success didn't come overnight, though. I vividly remember the first holiday meal I prepared. It was Easter Sunday, and I was cooking for eight: my husband and me, plus his parents and siblings. I started preparing a week in advance. When I unwrapped the half baby lamb I was going to serve, I had a meltdown and called my mom, grandma, and aunt to all come over to help. (Read about this enlightening experience on page 161.)

All of this is my way of telling you that it's *never* too late to learn to cook amazing food at home. If I could learn—when at age 21, I had yet to successfully use the stove—you can too.

The cover of this book promises that you will learn about the connection between business, leadership, and food. So, what of all that? You can find the beginnings of the answer to that question in an accounting classroom at Fordham University in New York City, where I've worked since 1987.

When I teach accounting, I always tell my students on the first day of the semester that the so-called "father of accounting," Luca Pacioli, was my distant cousin. In Italy in the 1400s, he became a scholar in mathematics and pursued innovations in double-entry bookkeeping that revolutionized the practice of accounting. My roots are in Italy, too (as you know, via the Bronx), and about 500 years after Pacioli made his mark, I became a professor of accounting and pursued innovations in business education that I hope someone will one day see as transformational in their own way.

I'm not sure whether Pacioli had any kitchen skills or even an interest in cooking, but as you now know, I do. Very much so. I've been on the lookout for intriguing connections between business and cooking ever since I mastered the stove.

Good accounting and good cooking have a lot in common. Accounting is essential to a harmonious business operation, and cooking is central to harmonious relationships among family and friends. Each requires attention to detail and, when it comes to both serving and tasting, honest disclosures.

Accounting and cooking have their complementary natures, too. Accounting appeals to my sense of calm—calling for order, with everything in its place—while cooking stirs my sense of creativity. Being creative brings me joy, and one of my greatest creative outlets is preparing things that people can eat and drink: cocktails, desserts, and, in the spirit of my mother and grandmother, full-on meals.

Like most first-generation Italian American college graduates, I chose my major based on the job I hoped to get. What drew me to business, and specifically to accounting, was the hope of a secure career path. I also knew I wanted to raise a family. A career teaching accounting met both needs. I was able to explore every facet of accounting that interested me while raising our three children and spending a reasonable number of hours at home.

So, as you can guess, this overlap between the joy of accounting and the joy of cooking is now a constant in my life. Both are primarily linear processes that lead to concrete outcomes. Both are part art, part science. Each sometimes requires rule-based action with absolute precision—such as calculating earnings per share or baking a delicate cake—and other times more interpretive judgment and estimation, such as when determining the useful life of an asset or deciding between baking versus frying your meatballs. (To me, frying adds the best flavor! See page 62 for my method, but always use your best judgment.)

When I became the dean of the business school at Fordham in 2007, I began noticing the parallels between cooking and leadership. I made connections between the ingredients I was using in meals and my work environment—ingredients that drove home so many lessons that made me a better leader. They also inspired the chapters you're about to read.

This book, part cookbook and part memoir, highlights the ties between what I do in the workplace and what I produce in the kitchen. Using the more than 100 recipes featured in these pages, you will learn to create dozens of full meals. Each chapter includes all of the elements: appetizers, main courses, side dishes, desserts, and beverage pairings. And each meal promises a good story! As you are reading and cooking, I encourage you to think about the role that food and drink play in your work and daily life. But mostly, I hope you enjoy preparing my recipes, sharing them at your dinner table (and perhaps with coworkers, too), and making new memories with family and friends.

Make Lemonade

1

Limoncello Champagne Cocktail
Shrimp Cocktail
Cocktail Sauce
Lemon Corn Soup
Gnocchi al Limone
Lemon Chicken Francese
Sautéed Spinach
Garlic Paste
Lemon Crumb Pie

*L*emons are a multiple-use asset: they are well-known for adding vitamin C, promoting healthy digestion, and some even say preventing cancer. Yet there are "lemon lists" for cars and investments that no one wants to be on. Good or bad, lemons have been a ubiquitous part of my life journey.

I can close my eyes and hear my grandmother saying, "Donna, when life hands you lemons—and it will!—make lemonade." It is ironic that I don't think she actually ever made lemonade, but time and time again, I watched her turn truly challenging situations into something palatable by preparing and serving delicious home-cooked meals.

I was a very curious child, continuously asking why. "Why can't I go?" "Why can't I stay up late?" "Why, why, why?!" When my mother reached her limit, she would often calmly respond to my latest "why" with, "Because a lemon died." It was her way of saying, "Stop asking and move on, because some things, my dear, will never have answers." Even into adulthood I wondered, how could a lemon die? I eventually found out.

As a graduate student in the 1980s, I studied George A. Akerlof's seminal paper, "The Market for 'Lemons': Quality Uncertainty and the Market Mechanism," which examined the damage that can be done to markets by asymmetric information. That's basically when one party in a transaction has access to more information than the other. *Reducing* asymmetric information—closing the knowledge gap between buyers and sellers, or between companies and investors—is a central goal of financial reporting and disclosures. Akerlof eventually won the Nobel Prize in Economics for his work in this area.

I recall lightening the mood during the comprehensive exam for my doctoral degree when I cited Akerlof's paper, reminding my team of faculty evaluators (the "investors" in my education) that this exam was their way to reduce asymmetric information, identify the best candidates, and weed out the lemons—the main point being, I was no lemon.

My evaluators got a kick out of my analogy, and I went on to pass the exam with high marks. Since then, I've realized that there are some cases when asymmetric information is actually a positive. For example, when the New York City Department of Health required that restaurants with over 200 locations add calorie counts to the menus. Sure, reducing asymmetric information gave buyers more information, but in this case, some didn't necessarily want it. For me, I'd rather see this sort of disclosure relegated to the footnotes.

I learned the hard way about one characteristic of lemons: their high level of citric acid that bestows a pleasant bite or tang to foods and drinks. The cook in me was pleased that lemons became a favorite of my three children; they squeezed them on everything, including their hands, and ate them right down to the rind. The mother in me, however, was less thrilled to discover the side effects of all that citric acid. In the mid-1990s, one of our daughters lathered her face and hands with a plate full of lemons and then went outside into the blazing summer sun. All the sunblock in the world couldn't have prevented her skin from burning to a crisp. Luckily, only her hand remains lightly scarred from that day. Funny enough, though, that experience influenced the way I cook fish. Squeezing lemon on the skin before broiling really crisps it.

Lemons continued to follow me in my travels. In 2007, while visiting the Isle of Capri, I found everything immensely picturesque: the Blue Grotto, the sea, the views. What really caught my attention, though, were all the lemon trees. They were everywhere, on the sides of mountains, all along the roadsides. They symbolized everything I found beautiful about Italy—the natural ingredients, the bright sun, the warmth, the simple yet fabulous meals, the joyful people.

After that trip, I convinced my family that we needed to have a lemon tree at our home. (Let me remind you that I lived and still live in New York, where the weather is not always warm and the people, well, not always joyful.) I ordered a free-standing, five-foot specimen from a farm in Italy. I watered it, I gave it direct sunlight, and I even talked to my beloved lemon tree, only to watch it wither away. It never produced even a single lemon.

While the tree never got its chance to impact my cooking, it did leave a lasting impression on the US Department of Agriculture. I had unwittingly brought it into the country illegally. Fortunately, by the time federal agents knocked on my door in the Bronx to retrieve it, it had long since fully depreciated and been turned into compost. I am now on my third lemon tree—entirely legal, I promise—and have finally learned that, yes, a lemon can indeed die.

My admiration for lemons continues to grow as my cooking skills advance. Lemon, while sour, can eliminate bitterness. It can also freshen up any number of drinks (see pages 7, 55, 100, 112). Squeeze lemon on your sautéed spinach (page 16) and it will take it to a whole new level.

The meals on the following pages can be prepared year round and are perfect for end-of-summer days. It makes the most of the culinary power of bright, bold, and effervescent lemons.

LIMONCELLO CHAMPAGNE COCKTAIL

Makes 1 cocktail

Prep Time: 5 minutes

This fizzy drink is super refreshing, and it far surpasses lemonade in terms of lifting your mood when life hands you lemons. When you pull your chilled champagne flute out of the freezer and mix up this lemony cocktail, you'll taste summer no matter what season it is. It reminds me of Italy, and I especially enjoy sipping on it outside in the sunshine.

Tips to make it great:

> Put the flute in the freezer for 15 minutes.
>
> Make sure the champagne is really cold and also chill the limoncello.

INGREDIENTS

- **2 ounces limoncello** (I like Caravella, but there are many great options)

- **6 ounces champagne** (I use Korbel when making champagne cocktails, but for a sweeter and less carbonated option, you can use Prosecco. La Marca is my go-to favorite.)

- **Sprig of mint**

INSTRUCTIONS

1. Chill the limoncello and champagne in the freezer for 1 hour.

2. Chill your champagne flute in the freezer for 15 minutes.

3. Remove the limoncello, champagne, and champagne flute from the freezer, and add 2 ounces of cold limoncello to the chilled flute.

4. Add the ice-cold champagne or Prosecco.

5. Top with a sprig of mint.

SHRIMP COCKTAIL

Serves 4 to 6

Prep Time: 10 to 15 minutes

Cook Time: 5 to 7 minutes

This simple recipe came to me via a cooking class I took with my husband and kids many years ago. The class was a gift they gave to me, but we were all a little anxious about cooking with complete strangers. For some reason, when they gave us name tags to fill out at the beginning of class, our son James wrote "Eugene" on his. One of the assistants at the cooking school took a liking to him and kept calling on "Eugene" throughout the class, which made us all laugh. To this day, when my son wants to remain incognito, he goes by Eugene.

Perfectly chilled shrimp always conjures up that fun and funny memory and makes me smile.

Tips to make it great:

Cook the thawed, uncleaned shrimp with the shell on.

Add cut lemons and peppercorns to the water before boiling.

After the shrimp turn pink, take them out and throw them in an ice bath immediately.

Note: *I use Himalayan pink salt in all of my recipes and recommend it highly.*
The exception is the salt I use to boil water.
In that case, add 1/4 cup of iodized salt to a 6-quart pot.

INGREDIENTS

3 tablespoons Himalayan pink salt or sea salt

1/4 cup black peppercorns

3 lemons, each sliced into 6 wedges, divided

2 pounds large shell-on fresh or frozen shrimp (8- to 10-count)

Romaine lettuce, for serving

1 cup Cocktail Sauce (page 10), **for serving**

INSTRUCTIONS

1. Fill a large pot three-quarters full with water. Add the salt, pepper, and 12 lemon wedges to it, and bring to a boil over high heat.

2. Prepare an ice-water bath in a large bowl (roughly 1 quart of ice and 1 quart of cold water).

3. Once the water is boiling, add the shrimp. Boil for 3 to 5 minutes.

4. When they've all turned pink and are rising to the top of the pot, remove them with a large slotted spoon or handled sieve. Transfer them to the ice bath to cool for about 1 minute.

5. Clean the shrimp. I use kitchen shears (you can buy seafood shears if you want to be extra fancy). Cut the back and peel the shell leaving a bit of the tail on. Run them under cold water, making sure to wash away the digestive tract. It isn't harmful if you eat it, but it's also not appetizing.

6. Drain and dry the shrimp. Place them in a covered bowl and refrigerate for at least 30 minutes until ready to serve.

7. Layer a bowl with leaves of your best-looking romaine lettuce and then place shrimp around the bowl. Arrange 6 lemon wedges between the shrimp. Place a small bowl of the Cocktail Sauce in the center of it all.

COCKTAIL SAUCE

Makes about 1 cup

Prep Time: 5 minutes

This is a very simple cocktail sauce that's easy to make, so you have no excuse not to! Once you make your own, you'll never buy the jarred stuff at the store again. It's never as tasty, and it costs too much.

INGREDIENTS

1/4 cup prepared horseradish

1/2 cup ketchup

2 teaspoons Frank's RedHot sauce

Juice from 1/2 lemon

INSTRUCTIONS

1. In a small bowl, combine everything and stir until fully incorporated. Use immediately or store tightly lidded in the refrigerator for up to a week.

LEMON CORN SOUP

Serves 4 to 6

Prep Time: 30 minutes

Cook Time: 30+ minutes

I enjoy preparing and eating soup all year long. This one is hearty enough to serve in the winter, but the fresh corn that's available in season makes it a summertime favorite with my family.

Tips to make it great:

Use fresh corn.

Add a dollop of sour cream to the bowl when serving.

INGREDIENTS

4 ears of corn

2 Yukon Gold potatoes cut into bite-size pieces

1 medium onion

1 can cannellini beans

5 cups chicken or vegetable stock

3 tablespoons lemon juice

Himalayan pink salt, to taste

Black or lemon pepper, to taste

INSTRUCTIONS

1. Clean the husks off the corn and then, using a knife, carefully remove the corn kernels and place them into a bowl. Remove 3 tablespoons of kernels and set aside.

2. Wash the potatoes and cut them into small chunks. Peel and chop the onion.

3. Working in batches, add about half of the corn, potatoes, onion, beans, and stock into the blender. Blend for 30 to 40 seconds, until the mixture is pureed. Pour into a 6-quart pot. Continue this process until you've pureed all the ingredients and added them to the large pot.

4. Add the lemon juice to the pot along with salt and pepper to taste and bring to a boil.

5. Once boiling, lower to a simmer for 5 minutes. At this point, add the corn kernels you had set aside to the pot of soup.

6. Cook on a low heat for an additional 30 minutes.

7. Serve with tortilla chips. My favorite are Tostitos. The salt and texture work really well together.

GNOCCHI AL LIMONE

Serves 4 to 6

Prep Time: 15 minutes

Cook Time: 25 minutes (most of this time is to cook the potatoes)

I'm usually not a fan of restaurant-prepared gnocchi, as they're often too dense and heavy. My husband has been known to call them "lead sinkers," which seems pretty spot-on to me. This recipe for gnocchi in lemon sauce, however, is quite different. We learned to make it from the chef at Casa Mele, a restaurant on Italy's Amalfi Coast. It's amazing, trust me! For the gnocchi, you cut the dough into tiny pieces and use a little less flour than usual, and they melt in your mouth.

Tips to make it great:

Make sure the lemons are fresh.

Putting the potatoes through the ricer requires some hand strength. So, make this with a friend and take turns mashing.

Put on some Italian music while you prepare the recipe and enjoy a glass of Pinot Grigio.

INGREDIENTS

2 pounds Yukon Gold potatoes

1 extra large egg

3 1/2 cups all-purpose flour, plus more for dusting

INSTRUCTIONS

1 Fill a large pot with cold water. After rinsing the potatoes, put them in the pot unpeeled and simmer for about 20 to 25 minutes, depending on the size of the potatoes, until they are cooked through. You should be able to easily slice the potato in half once done.

INGREDIENTS (cont.)

1/2 teaspoon Himalayan pink salt

1 stick Kerrygold salted butter (or any salted butter)

1 cup fresh heavy cream

Zest of lemon, to taste

2 tablespoons iodized salt for boiling water

Parmigiano-Reggiano, to taste

INSTRUCTIONS (cont.)

2   Strain and set aside to cool. Once the potatoes are cool enough to touch, peel them, then mash them using a potato ricer or other tool.

3   Put small amounts of the soft potato into the ricer, and squeeze them through. Transfer the "riced" potatoes to a large bowl and continue until all the potatoes have been put through the ricer.

4   Next add the egg, flour, and Himalayan pink salt to the bowl of riced potatoes. Mix well. Sprinkle flour on your clean countertop and break the dough into 4 or 5 pieces.

5   Taking one piece at a time, roll on the countertop into a worm (I always get flashbacks of Play-Doh). Cut the worm into small pieces no bigger than 1/4 inch wide. Keep plenty of flour on the countertop. Repeat with the rest of the dough. Working in batches, transfer the gnocchi to a colander and shake off the excess flour. Set aside.

6   Fill a pot with water and bring to a boil. Add 2 tablespoons of iodized salt to the water. Put the gnocchi in the boiling water for about 7 minutes until they rise to the top.

7   Meanwhile, mix the butter, cream, and lemon zest in a bowl. Once mixed, transfer to a small sauté pan and simmer for approximately 5 minutes until the cream reduces.

8   Using a strainer, remove the cooked gnocchi from the boiling water and transfer them to the sauté pan. Gently stir for 1 to 2 minutes. Sprinkle with Parmigiano-Reggiano and additional lemon zest.

LEMON CHICKEN FRANCESE

Serves 4 to 6

Prep Time: 20 minutes

Cook Time: 20 minutes

This one is a favorite of all three of my children. It was a dish I could make every night when they were growing up and no one would complain. If you are a parent of more than one child, you know what a beautiful and rare thing that is.

Tips to make it great:

Use small, thin pieces of chicken or veal.

Use drinking wine rather than cooking wine.
I like using Santa Margarita Pinot Grigio.

INGREDIENTS

2 extra large eggs

1 cup all-purpose flour

3 tablespoons garlic powder

Himalayan pink salt, to taste

Black pepper, to taste

6 chicken cutlets (I generally buy Bell & Evans)

Extra-virgin olive oil, for sautéing and finishing

1/2 stick butter

1 cup chicken stock or 1/2 cup of chicken stock and 1/2 cup of Pinot Grigio

Sprig of parsley

1/2 cup lemon juice

2 lemons

INSTRUCTIONS

1. Beat the eggs in a bowl large enough to dip the chicken in and set aside. Place the flour in a separate bowl large enough to dip the chicken in and set aside.

2. Season the chicken cutlets with the garlic powder, salt, and pepper. Dredge each cutlet in the flour, then dip into the beaten eggs and lay on a plate.

3. Sauté the dredged cutlets in a large pan over medium heat in olive oil until just about fully cooked, then set aside.

4. After cleaning the frying pan, melt half a stick of butter with 2 tablespoons of olive oil. Add in the chicken stock, parsley, and lemon juice. Once it comes to a low boil, add the pre-sautéed chicken cutlets to the pan, turning them after 1 minute.

5. Place the sliced lemons into the pan and cook for another 2 to 3 minutes. If your pan isn't large enough to hold all six cutlets, do this in batches.

6. As an alternative, you can use veal cutlets. Note that veal will cook more quickly.

SAUTÉED SPINACH

Makes 4 to 6 servings

Prep Time: 5 minutes • Cook Time: 5 minutes

If you don't love spinach, this might be the recipe to change your mind. It's so simple, but it has layers of flavor from the Homemade Garlic Paste (page 17), freshly squeezed lemon, and Himalayan pink salt.

Tip to make it great:

> Remember that fresh spinach cooks quickly and keeps cooking even after you take it off the stove.

INGREDIENTS

2 8-ounce packages of spinach (can also be purchased loose or in unpackaged bunches)

Garlic Paste (see recipe on next page)

Extra-virgin olive oil, to sauté

1/2 lemon

Himalayan pink salt, to taste

Black pepper, to taste

INSTRUCTIONS

1   Wash the spinach and drain thoroughly.

2   In a large frying pan with a lid, sauté the garlic paste with olive oil. Once the oil is hot, add the spinach. Its volume will be greater than the size of the pan, but it will reduce quickly, so you can add in batches if needed.

3   Cooking the spinach will take less than 5 minutes. Remove from heat and squeeze a lemon all over the cooked spinach. Add salt and pepper to taste.

4   You can serve this spinach as a side dish or add it to the Lemon Corn Soup (page 10) to give it some additional texture.

GARLIC PASTE

Makes about 8 ounces

Prep Time: 5 minutes

If you don't already make your own garlic paste, now you can. You're welcome! It's easy to make and will keep, tightly sealed, in your refrigerator for two to three weeks.

INGREDIENTS

2 whole cloves of garlic

2 to 3 tablespoons extra-virgin olive oil

INSTRUCTIONS

1   Peel the garlic cloves and place them in a food processor, ideally a miniature one or one with a small-sized bowl. Add olive oil and process for 30 to 40 seconds or until completely smooth.

2   Put in a small container with a lid (a glass jar is best) and refrigerate.

LEMON CRUMB PIE

Makes 8 to 10 servings

Prep Time: 20 minutes

Cook Time: 40 minutes

Lemon pie has been described as one of most popular desserts in the United States. It's certainly been around for a long time. An American chef is credited with penning the first lemon pie recipe way back in 1806. I turn a fairly traditional lemon pie into something really special with my signature crumb topping.

Tips to make it great:

The ratio of these ingredients varies depending on the recipe, but the basic principles are always the same. The acidity of the lemon juice interacts with the eggs and cornstarch to create a thick, creamy filling. Sugar offsets the tartness of the lemon juice and provides sweetness. You can use a little more or a little less depending on your taste.

Get someone to help mix when it's time to make the crumbs or use a food processor.

Pie Crust

I must confess that I use frozen pie crust so I can focus on the filling and crumbs.

1 9-inch pre-made pie shell

Pie Filling

INGREDIENTS

1/2 cup granulated sugar

1 teaspoon cornstarch

2 extra large eggs

1 lemon, zest and then set aside for juicing

1 cup hot water

INSTRUCTIONS

1 Preheat the oven to 375 degrees F.

2 In a medium bowl, whisk together the granulated sugar and cornstarch. Add the eggs and beat the mixture well. Beat in the lemon juice and zest until well blended. Stir in the hot water and set aside to cool while you prepare the crumb topping.

Crumb Topping
(This is the tedious part!)

INGREDIENTS

1/2 cup granulated sugar

3/4 cup all-purpose flour

1/2 stick thoroughly softened butter (not melted)

1 teaspoon baking powder

Pinch of Himalayan pink salt

INSTRUCTIONS

1 Add the granulated sugar, flour, softened butter, baking powder, and salt to a large mixing bowl and stir until the mix crumbs. This can take about 10 minutes, so stick with it. I alternate between a fork and a spoon. Once you have fine crumbs, set aside.

Assembly

1 Pour the filling into the pie shell and sprinkle the crumbs evenly over the top.

2 Bake for 30 minutes, then cover the pie with aluminum foil and bake for 10 more minutes (total baking time = 40 minutes).

3 Cool completely before enjoying.

2

Pass the Cheese

Vodka Martini with Blue Cheese Olives

Artichoke, Cheese, and Spinach Dip

Giambelli's Gondolette alla Panna

Veal Chop Caprese

Goat Cheese Beet Salad

Cheesecake

For as long as I can remember, I've enjoyed adding all kinds of cheeses to my recipes (*and* eating it outside the context of those recipes). It's amazing that only four simple ingredients are needed to make natural cheese: milk, salt, a starter culture, and an enzyme called rennet. In the hands of experts, these raw materials transform into an array of what we call in the business world "perishable inventory." Whether blue, hard, semi-hard, semi-soft, or another of cheese's fascinating and widely varied categories, it's a global favorite.

I do apologize at the outset if you've come here looking for a cheese recipe. I've never made my own cheese, but I did have a cousin who did (I miss you, Ray). I've also watched in awe, on many occasions, as Sicilian native Orazio Carciotto makes mouthwatering mozzarella at his Bronx shop, Casa Della Mozzarella.

Though I've never produced a cheese from scratch, cheese has added untold value to a multitude of my recipes. It's also given me a deeper understanding of three important concepts in the business world: teamwork, change, and persistence. Cheese (in particular, American cheese) is a food that conjures up the business concept of teamwork, along with my dad and the New York Yankees.

My dad swore he "almost" made the Yankees' team in the 1950s. He always kept a card in his wallet that stated he participated in the 1955 tryouts. I was super impressed, as was everyone to whom he showed the card. Later in life, my awe wore off when I learned that my dad's brother, my uncle Vinny, had the very same card. I began to wonder if everyone on their block was invited to the Yankees tryouts.

That card represents my earliest childhood memory of the Yankees, but countless family tales are also associated with the team. One of those stories—and the life lessons it imparted—is tied directly to cheese.

My father grew up in the Fort Apache area of the Bronx, and Yankees games were a big part of his life. He often went with the same group of friends, and they had a routine with the stadium concessions. Mike would buy the hot dogs, my dad would get the beer, Joe would grab the ice cream. It was an unspoken rule that each person who stood in line would get enough for everyone in the group. One particular day, after my father and all his friends had enjoyed the concession items, another friend they'd brought along, Vic, pulled a cheese sandwich—American on white bread—from his bag and started to eat it. My dad looked over and in a deadly serious tone asked Vic, "Where's my cheese sandwich?" What was also implied was, "Where is Joe's cheese sandwich? And Mike's?"

Vic answered that he'd only made one for himself, saying he didn't think anybody else would want one, and that he only had enough cheese at home for one sandwich anyway. The group wasn't pleased. My father always envisioned his Yankees buddies as a team, and he believed that everyone should be a contributing member.

With his usual mix of humor and directness, my father decided he would make four cheese sandwiches and bring them over to Vic's house to reinforce the importance of sharing. Before dropping them off, he learned that Vic and his family wouldn't be there to accept the delivery—they'd left town for Puerto Rico. My dad spent the rest of the day figuring out how to get the point across to Vic that when you're part of a team, you take care of the team.

Ultimately, he took four extremely well-wrapped American cheese sandwiches to the Federal Express office and shipped them to the El San Juan hotel where Vic and his family were staying. He included a note saying that for a team to succeed, every member should contribute.

Perhaps it's no surprise, then, in the spirit of my dad, that I associate cheese with persistence. My first real experience with baking—and by "real" I mean free of Betty Crocker's influence—was as a newlywed. My husband and I were invited to his aunt's house for a meal with his grandmother. I decided it would be important to show my new family that I was a good baker, which was not true.

I thought about a cheesecake that a friend often prepared for parties. Asking her to make the cheesecake for me would have defeated the purpose, so I asked for the recipe. If you've never made cheesecake, it's like a private equity investment: the ingredients are expensive, and it takes time. I found out the hard way that it's not a risk-free investment, either.

After laboring to put together my very first cheesecake, I watched through the oven window as the surface of the cake, which was meant to be perfectly smooth, cracked into a depressing mosaic. For help, I appealed to my friend, who revealed that she'd forgotten to tell me to put the cake pan into a water bath and to leave the oven door halfway open for a quarter of the four-hour baking process. I gathered all of my strength (and another batch of ingredients) and tried again. The second version looked great!

Filled with pride, I carried the finished product into my husband's aunt's house. Nanny, his 90-year-old grandmother, tasted it, smiled, and told me in Italian, "You need to keep trying, and it will be better next time." That wasn't *exactly* what I wanted to hear, but I was not deterred. I continued to make cheesecake many times in the years to follow, and ultimately, I achieved something delicious.

Cheese became a metaphor for change for me when I read the 1998 classic business book that has its name in the title. Maybe you've heard of *Who Moved My Cheese?: An Amazing Way to Deal with Change in Your Work and in Your Life* by Dr. Spencer Johnson. The fun fable illustrates the difficult and yet essential nature of change. In it, cheese is code for what businesses and people seek in life: for companies, success, and for humans, happiness. Through an allegory about two mice and two tiny humans who live inside a maze, and whose life trajectories are centered on cheese, Spencer explores how our desires may prompt us to embrace, ignore, or resist change, and why adaptation and flexibility are key to getting what we want.

The main takeaway still sticks with me: Even if we fight change, it will still happen. Companies and people that seek change as part of their strategy will ultimately end up with the greatest array of options—and lots of the proverbial cheese. In business, life, and food preparation, if cheese is what you want, you need to be anticipatory and adaptable.

These themes came to life for me most vividly between 2013 and 2015, when Fordham University set its sights on an especially exciting piece of "cheese": the unification of our undergraduate and graduate schools of business into one cohesive institution. We had our very own equivalents of the iconic characters from Spencer's book: Sniffs and Scurrys, motivated by instinct and ready to move forward; and Hems and Haws, governed by sentiments and emotions, some of whom were skeptical and even obstructionistic.

All of us worked together to find a way to achieve change, and today, the unified Gabelli School of Business educates more than 4,000 students at once across its bachelor's, master's, doctoral, and executive education programs.

Actual cheese provided an interesting side lesson in the Gabelli School's unification, too, when it came to the costs and benefits of outsourcing. As we worked to build a new structure and culture for one school, we had many all-day work sessions and team-building workshops, some of which ended in dinners or cocktail parties to celebrate milestones. When the bills from the university's in-house caterer arrived, I was shocked to see what we were being charged for the mediocre cheese platters, which were mostly crackers.

I was encouraged to look into outsourcing the staff celebrations to local restaurants, and it turned out that it was much more fun (and significantly less costly, even in midtown Manhattan) to hold the parties outside of the office. The lessons in cheese are never-ending!

The recipes I've included in this chapter illustrate how various cheeses can be combined to form a team of delicious flavors. For dessert, I've included a creamy cheesecake recipe (with that cheese persistence lesson I learned!) that will help you to build perseverance in the kitchen.

By adding cheese to a recipe, you always change its flavor—sometimes dramatically, as in my Veal Chop Caprese on page 29, and other times more subtly, as in my daughter Danielle's Goat Cheese Beet Salad on page 31. With cheese, as in life, change is a constant. So, let's not fight it and be friends with it instead—for the love of cheese!

VODKA MARTINI WITH BLUE CHEESE OLIVES

Makes 1 cocktail

Prep Time: 5 minutes

There is really nothing like a well-made martini to kick off a special dinner. People may debate whether a martini is best shaken or stirred, or dry or dirty (our son James has been accused of drinking the olive juice all by itself). But in our house, there is no debate about one thing: If the cocktail shaker is out and filled with ice, with the requisite vodka and vermouth ready to be tipped in, the whole evening might deflate if one opens up the fridge to find that there are no blue cheese olives.

Tips to make it great:

> Have a lot of ice on hand.
>
> Put the martini glass in the freezer for 15 minutes.
>
> Make sure all ingredients are very cold.

INGREDIENTS

2 olives stuffed with blue cheese (I use DeLallo Blue Cheese-Stuffed Olives, which come in a jar, but you can stuff your own olives as well)

1 ounce dry vermouth

3 ounces Grey Goose vodka or Stolichnaya Elit vodka (or any vodka of your choice)

INSTRUCTIONS

1 Place a martini glass in the freezer as you gather ingredients.

2 Put two blue-cheese-stuffed olives on a long toothpick and set aside.

3 Once the glass is chilled, take it out of the freezer and fill it with ice.

4 In a shaker, add more ice, the dry vermouth, and vodka.

5 Let it stand for 1 minute, then shake well for about 1 minute. Empty the ice from the martini glass and pour the mixed cocktail from the shaker into the chilled glass. Add the olive-pierced toothpick.

ARTICHOKE, CHEESE, AND SPINACH DIP

Makes 6 to 8 servings

Prep Time: 10 minutes • Cook Time: 20 minutes

My children and their friends always loved the artichoke spinach dip at TGI Fridays, so when I saw it one day in the frozen section of the grocery store, I purchased it. They were super excited. But after I read the list of ingredients on the box, many of which I couldn't pronounce, I decided it was time for me to learn how to make it. It's been a family favorite ever since.

Tips to make it great:

Use fresh spinach, and make sure you squeeze all the water out of it after cooking (you can wrap the cooked spinach in a few layers of paper towels to wring out all the liquid).

This dip tastes best when you use jarred marinated artichoke hearts.

Provide a bunch of dipping options: Tostitos, bagel chips, bread, pretzels.

INGREDIENTS

8 ounces spinach

Cooking oil spray, to coat

8 ounces softened cream cheese

1 cup sour cream

3/4 cup marinated artichoke hearts

1 teaspoon Garlic Paste (see page 17)

1/2 teaspoon Himalayan pink salt

INSTRUCTIONS

1 Preheat the oven to 375 degrees F.

2 In a medium pan over medium heat, sauté the spinach until wilted. Let cool, wring out the excess water, and coarsely chop.

3 Add the cream cheese, sour cream, cooked spinach, artichoke hearts, garlic paste, salt, pepper, Parmigiano-Reggiano, and half of the mozzarella (3/4 cup) to a pot and warm all ingredients. Stir until well combined.

(continued on next page)

INGREDIENTS (cont.)

Black pepper, to taste

1/2 cup Parmigiano-Reggiano

1 1/2 cups shredded mozzarella, divided

INSTRUCTIONS (cont.)

4   Coat a small baking dish with cooking spray. Spread the spinach mixture into the prepared dish. Top with the remaining 3/4 cup of mozzarella.

5   Bake for 20 minutes, or until the dip is bubbly and the top layer of cheese is melted. Then broil for 2 to 3 more minutes, or until the top layer of cheese lightly browns.

GIAMBELLI'S GONDOLETTE ALLA PANNA

Makes 6 to 8 servings

Prep Time: 1 hour • Cook Time: 10 minutes

The owner of Giambelli 50th Ristorante, Francesco Giambelli, gave me this recipe for pasta pillows filled with a mixture of five kinds of cheese more than 30 years ago. He proudly told me that it was a favorite of Pope John Paul II, whom he served during his 1995 visit to New York City. Sadly, the restaurant closed in 2009, but the beautiful meals and memories, including my 40th birthday celebration, are forever. And, of course, so is this recipe.

Tips to make it great:

This recipe requires precision and exact measurements, much like calculating earnings per share. Follow the steps exactly, and everyone will have the same outcome.

As noted below, allow a full hour for preparation before you are ready to start cooking the pasta.

Filling

INGREDIENTS

1/2 cup **Parmigiano-Reggiano**

1/2 cup **fontina**

1/2 cup **cream cheese**

1/2 cup **ricotta**

1/2 cup **mascarpone**

1/2 cup **boiled spinach**

1/4 **onion, sliced thin and sautéed until brown**

Pinch of Himalayan pink salt

Pinch of pepper

INSTRUCTIONS

1 Put all the filling ingredients into the blender and blend for 4 minutes until fully incorporated. Set aside.

Dough

INGREDIENTS

1 pound **all-purpose flour, plus more for dusting**

3 **extra large egg yolks**

3 **extra large eggs**

1 tablespoon **extra-virgin olive oil**

1/4 cup **water**

Himalayan pink salt, to taste

INSTRUCTIONS

1 In a large bowl, mix all of the ingredients together for 20 minutes to ensure that they are fully combined.

2 Roll the dough until it is paper thin using a flour-dusted rolling pin and cut into 3-by-3-inch squares.

(continued on next page)

Forming and Boiling the Gondolette

1 Put 1 tablespoon of filling in the center of each square of dough. Fold into a triangle or pyramid shape by bringing all four corners upward and crimping the edges together.

2 Boil a large pot of salted water. To prevent the gondolette from breaking, place them in a hand-held sieve and cook them by immersing the sieve in the boiling water for 5 minutes.

3 Remove the sieve from the water and transfer the gondolette to a paper towel–lined plate to dry. If you are using a small sieve, you can do this step in batches.

Sauce

INGREDIENTS

2 cups heavy cream

1/2 cup whipped butter

1/2 cup grated Parmigiano-Reggiano

Salt and pepper, to taste

INSTRUCTIONS

1 While the gondolette are boiling, place a large (16-inch) skillet over another burner. In it, combine the heavy cream and whipped butter. Cook over medium heat. Once the butter is 95 percent melted, add the Parmigiano and stir for a few seconds.

2 Place the boiled gondolette in the skillet and simmer for 2 minutes.

Serve immediately.

Note: I have also served these pasta pillows with Sunday Gravy (page 60) and Marinara Sauce (page 190).

VEAL CHOP CAPRESE

Makes 2 servings

Prep Time: 30 minutes • Cook Time: 15 minutes

Veal is a family favorite just about any way I prepare it, ranging from simple cutlets to veal with peppers. This rendition, however, is at the top of everyone's list. The beauty of its Italian colors—red, white, and green—is only outdone by the full flavors. Your family and friends will be inviting themselves back for you to prepare it again quite soon, perhaps next week!

Tips to make it great:

> Get fresh mozzarella from a local deli rather than the supermarket.
>
> Don't overcook the veal chop—it is best if served pink.

INGREDIENTS

2 extra large eggs

3 tablespoons whole milk

Splash of club soda or sparkling water

1/2 cup seasoned breadcrumbs

2 veal chops

1/2 cup extra-virgin olive oil (half for frying and the other half for dressing the salad)

1/2 cup mozzarella, cubed

3/4 cup cherry tomatoes, quartered

INSTRUCTIONS

1 Preheat the oven to 350 degrees F.

2 In a medium bowl large enough to dip the veal chops, crack the eggs and add the milk and splash of club soda. Beat together.

3 On a flat platter, evenly spread out the breadcrumbs.

4 Dip each veal chop into the egg mixture, ensuring that every part is coated. Dip each chop into the breadcrumbs to completely cover. Place the coated chops on a clean plate and set aside.

(continued on next page)

INGREDIENTS (cont.)

1 sprig fresh parsley, chopped

4 tablespoons balsamic vinegar

Juice from 1 lemon, divided

1/4 cup finely grated Parmigiano-Reggiano

INSTRUCTIONS (cont.)

5   Pour half the olive oil (1/4 cup) into a large skillet and heat over medium-high heat until sizzling. I usually drop a bit of the breadcrumbs in to be sure the oil is hot enough.

6   Once the oil is hot, brown the chops in the pan until the breadcrumbs look cooked, about 2 minutes on each side.

7   Place the chops on a paper towel–lined plate to remove any excess oil. After patting down the chops, place them in a baking dish and transfer to the oven to bake for 15 minutes.

8   While the chops are baking, prepare the caprese topping. In a medium bowl, combine the mozzarella, tomato, and parsley. In a small bowl for the salad dressing, combine the remaining olive oil, balsamic vinegar, and the juice from one half of the lemon. Add the dressing to the mozzarella bowl and mix well.

9   When the chops are cooked, let them rest at room temperature for 5 minutes. Then, using a spoon, place some of the topping onto each chop, along with a quick squeeze of juice from the other half of your lemon, and finish each chop with a sprinkle of Parmigiano-Reggiano.

GOAT CHEESE BEET SALAD

Makes 6 to 8 servings

Prep Time: 15 minutes • Cook Time: 20 minutes

(if you are boiling or roasting the beets fresh)

My daughter Danielle turned me on to this delicious recipe. She failed to tell me, however, to roast or boil the beets before peeling. I tried using a potato peeler on the raw beets and ended up peeling my knuckles. Ouch! I have since invested in anti-slip "potato gloves" that I use to peel warm beets as well as potatoes.

Tips to make it great:

Fresh beets really are better, especially if you mix red and yellow.

Use gloves! Some stores sell reusable "potato gloves," but disposable food gloves are fine too. While the beets are still hot, rub the skin off using your hands, and then put the beets in cold water.

If you prefer, you can use ready-to-eat beets, which are boiled and peeled already. Thanks to a recommendation from one of my mom's friends, I have successfully used Gefen Organic Beets on a number of occasions.

INGREDIENTS

6 whole medium beets

1/2 cup extra-virgin olive oil

Himalayan pink salt and black pepper, to taste

1 (16-ounce) carton cherry tomatoes

1/4 cup balsamic vinegar

1/2 cup crumbled goat cheese

INSTRUCTIONS

1 To cook the beets, boil them in a large pot filled with water for approximately 20 minutes. Poke them with a fork to make sure they are cooked. I like them firm but not hard. Once cooked through, peel them (see above).

2 Cut the peeled beets into bite-size pieces. Transfer them to a large bowl and drizzle with half of the olive oil and salt and pepper to taste.

3 Cut the cherry tomatoes into quarters and place on top of the beets in bowl. Drizzle the rest of the olive oil and balsamic vinegar on top. Let sit for 15 minutes. Add goat cheese, stir to combine, and serve.

CHEESECAKE

Makes 8 to 10 servings

Prep Time: 20 minutes, then rest for 1 hour and refrigerate for 2 hours

Cook Time: 45 minutes

As you read in the chapter introduction, it took me a while to get this recipe right, but it was well worth the extra effort—you'll see! If the top of the cake cracks, ignore the cracks or cover them with a few sliced fresh strawberries. I discourage you from using canned fruit, though, because it detracts from the flavor of the cake.

Tips to make it great:

Follow the directions precisely.

Place the cheesecake pan in a roasting pan half filled with water.

Leave the cake in the oven for one hour after it's cooked with the oven off and the oven door open. This should prevent cracking.

Graham Cracker Crust

INGREDIENTS

15 graham cracker squares

2 tablespoons granulated sugar

3 tablespoons melted butter

INSTRUCTIONS

1 Preheat the oven to 350 degrees F.

2 Crush the graham crackers into crumbs by using a blender or putting them in a sealed bag and crushing them with a rolling pin. (You can sometimes also purchase a box of graham cracker crumbs at the supermarket.)

3 Add them to a medium bowl, then add the sugar and butter and stir everything until it forms a paste-like consistency.

INSTRUCTIONS (cont.)

4   Line the bottom of a 9-inch springform pan with the crust mixture and bake for 10 minutes. Remove from oven and set aside to cool.

5   Lower the oven temperature to 300 degrees F.

Cheesecake Filling

INGREDIENTS

3 extra large eggs

3 (8-ounce) packages cream cheese at room temperature

2 cups sour cream

1 cup granulated sugar

1/2 teaspoon vanilla extract

1 teaspoon freshly squeezed lemon juice

INSTRUCTIONS

1   In a medium bowl, and using an electric mixer, combine all of the filling ingredients until all lumps are gone. Don't overmix, and don't mix on too high of a speed, which can over-aerate the filling.

2   Pour the filling into the baked crust.

3   The cheesecake pan will bake in a water bath. Fill a roasting pan halfway with water and place the springform pan in the center of the water bath. Place into the oven and bake at 300 degrees F for 45 minutes. If top of cake starts to get too brown, cover with foil.

4   Turn the oven off and open the door halfway. Leave the cheesecake inside the oven in its water bath for an additional hour. Remove from the oven and allow to cool completely at room temperature. Then refrigerate for 2 hours before serving.

Surprise, It's Duck

Fluffy Duck

Duck and Goat Cheese Crostini

Bucatini Pasta with Duck Bolognese

Roast Duck aka Peking Duck

Sautéed Mushrooms with Duck

Orange Creme Brulée with Duck Eggs

*D*ucks can swim and fly, and some scientists believe they may even be capable of abstract thought. In general, duck behavior signals to me the unexpected and amazing. I feel the same way about the range of culinary preparations you can accomplish with duck.

The lessons I've learned from ducks started early in my life, beginning with the joy of inhaling helium from a party balloon and laughing and talking like that famous duck we all knew from cartoons. Doing that for the first time led to a feeling of absolute surprise.

That feeling of surprise re-emerged years later on my honeymoon in Paris when I ordered duck for dinner, receiving what looked like a filet mignon rather than a roast poultry-looking dish. My immediate assumption was that I'd ordered something other than duck in my attempt at French, but what was on my plate was indeed moulard duck—quite pink and truly amazing. That same night, I watched in surprise as all the women in the restaurant enjoyed cigars, solidifying my association of duck with new things.

Next, duck helped me learn the difference between empathy and sympathy. As we enjoyed duck during an extended-family meal, I consoled my young cousin who was crying hysterically at the table, concerned that we were eating Donald Duck. I felt for her and wanted to help. I also had no problem eating my share. Donald Duck was delicious.

My associations between duck and the world of business came later. The first time I connected ducks to accounting was early in my career as a college professor in the 1990s. I was doing research that piqued my interest in the differences between the accounting methods used in the United States and the United Kingdom (both known as Generally Accepted Accounting Principles in their respective countries). This research introduced me to the work of Sir David Tweedie, an incredibly dynamic and funny person (not your typical accountant) who chaired the UK's accounting standards board and went on to lead the International Accounting Standards Board for a decade, starting in 2001.

Tweedie used a "duck test" to illustrate the superiority of one set of accounting principles, which emphasize substance rather than form, over another set of accounting principles that focus on rules. As complex financial instruments emerged into the market, often bearing labels that misrepresented their nature, he used the "duck test" to distinguish between debt (which a company is required to pay back) and equity (no obligation for repayment), even if a lengthy description said otherwise.

"If it looks like a duck, walks like a duck, and quacks like a duck, it is a duck," he famously said (or at least famously among accountants). "What we do not need is a comprehensive scientific treatise on waterfowl, recounting the domestic habits of mallard, goldeneye, and teal, and explaining at length the precise genetic characteristics that differentiate ducks, swans, and geese."

The duck test has helped me to trust my direct observations, generally serving me well in both my professional and personal life. But I always remember that even if it looks like a duck, walks like a duck, and quacks like a duck, it could be a loot or a coot.

I am not sure which of two factors first made me aware of the many leadership lessons we can and should learn from ducks: the "The Mighty Ducks" movies, which my children watched dozens of times, or a colleague who was an avid duck hunter.

In the movies, Emilio Estevez, who played the namesake hockey team's coach, encouraged his players to skate in a V-shaped formation like the one in which ducks fly, with each duck taking a turn as the leader and the whole group working together as a team. My children would quack excitedly when the players made the V, perhaps for good reason: research shows that the lead position isn't necessarily the most strenuous and that the team approach adds 70 percent more flying range over what one bird could do alone.

Meanwhile, my hunter colleague shared that ducks tend not to leave their fellow travelers behind, circling back if a member of their group has been shot, even if it causes others to be killed. An admirable quality leading to such grave harm gave me a lot to think about. At least for the Mighty Ducks, this strategy worked out great.

For me, duck also drives home the lesson of coming together. One of my favorite dishes is Peking duck or, as they call it in Beijing, roast duck. I discovered this style of cooking duck in my early 20s in New York City's Chinatown, first at a restaurant plainly called Peking Duck, and later at its sister establishment, Peking Duck West. Later, we became regulars at Chin Chin, where they served amazing Peking Duck.

The crispy skin, hoisin sauce, fresh scallion, and cucumber create a taste that is unforgettable. You can imagine my excitement, then, when I took my first trip to Beijing in 2010 for a Fordham University work commitment. Alongside meetings with colleagues from Peking University, trying local Peking duck was on my agenda.

My hosts from the university were beyond gracious. They met me at the airport, planned all my professional meetings, and took me to a nearby section of the Great Wall of China and a tea house. I was amazed by their kindness, but also shocked by the lack of duck on the menus of any places we visited. After a busy week of meetings (punctuated by feelings of frustration at my inability to log into my Gmail), I was ready to give up on the duck.

I put the thought aside and headed to a dinner at Quan Jude restaurant with deans and distinguished professors from Peking University, some of whom were involved with political affairs in

Beijing. We sat at a large round table that featured a lazy Susan in the center, filled with an array of foods. I didn't know what all of them were, but I tried each one as the members of the Peking University delegation spoke freely about the challenges China was facing, along with their fears and hopes. It was around this table that I felt a total connection with them.

It was also around this time that the dish I had been waiting for landed on the lazy Susan: roast duck! I was full by that point, but you know I made room and was not disappointed. I have visited China nearly a dozen times since then, and I always make sure to have the roast duck. I'm also always struck by the hospitality I am shown and the candor and connection that unfold during a meal in China. I keep in touch with my colleagues there, and their hospitality remains an unexpected source of support.

I hope these recipes both surprise and delight you.

FLUFFY DUCK

Makes 1 cocktail

Prep Time: 5 minutes

This refreshing, creamy rum drink is great to serve either before or after dinner. It's not only fun but it is an engaging conversation starter.

Tips to make it great:

Have a lot of ice on hand and make sure all the ingredients are well chilled.

Serve in a chilled martini glass.

Garnish with a tablespoon of whipped cream.

INGREDIENTS

1 ounce white rum (I use Bacardi)

1 ounce advocaat (a traditional creamy eggnog-like Dutch alcohol available at most liquor stores)

1 ounce half-and-half

1 tablespoon whipped cream

INSTRUCTIONS

1. Place a martini glass in the freezer as you gather ingredients.

2. Take the chilled glass out of the freezer and fill it with ice.

3. In a shaker, put more ice, the rum, advocaat, and half-and-half.

4. Let stand for one minute, then shake well for about 1 minute. Discard the ice and pour the cocktail from the shaker into the martini glass. Garnish with the whipped cream.

Note: A more traditional beverage pairing with the recipes in this section is a glass or two of your favorite Barolo wine. Marcarini is a label I enjoy.

DUCK AND GOAT CHEESE CROSTINI

Makes 6 servings

Prep Time: 15 minutes

Cook Time: 15 minutes

Crostini is a wonderful appetizer that I enjoy preparing in a variety of ways. It can be as simple as a ricotta or tomato crostini. This special recipe is worth the extra effort, and it melts in your mouth. (See page 131 for two additional crostini recipes.)

Tips to make it great:

Use a meat thermometer.

Let the duck sit for 10 to 12 minutes before slicing it.

(continued on next page)

INGREDIENTS

12 pieces of thinly sliced French bread

1/4 cup plus 1 tablespoon extra-virgin olive oil

Himalayan pink salt, to season

1 (12-ounce) duck breast

1/2 cup goat cheese

1/4 cup whole milk

1/3 cup heavy cream

INSTRUCTIONS

1   Preheat the oven to 350 degrees F.

2   Using a pastry brush, rub each side of each piece of bread generously with the olive oil, and sprinkle each side with a pinch of salt. Transfer to a baking sheet and bake for 5 minutes. Flip and cook for 3 to 5 more minutes, or until crispy. (This step can be done in advance if needed.)

3   Increase the oven temperature to 400 degrees F.

4   Slice the duck breast into 3 pieces on an angle and season generously with salt. Place the duck skin side down into a cold pan on the stovetop and cook over low heat for 5 minutes. Flip the duck and cook for 2 minutes. Remove it from the pan.

5   Place a wire rack on a baking tray and transfer the duck pieces to the wire rack, skin side up. This will catch any grease that drips off the duck while it bakes. Bake for 5 to 7 minutes, or until the internal temperature on a meat thermometer reads 125 degrees F.

6   Remove the duck from the oven and set aside to rest for 10 to 12 minutes, then cut it into 12 thin slices.

Goat Cheese Spread

In a medium bowl, mix the goat cheese and milk together until smooth. In a separate bowl, whip the cream to soft peaks, and then stir it into the goat cheese mixture.

Assembly

Place a spoonful of the goat cheese mix onto each crostini, followed by a slice of duck breast. Serve and enjoy!

BUCATINI PASTA WITH DUCK BOLOGNESE

Makes 4 servings

Prep Time: 15 minutes • Cook Time: 30 minutes

Bolognese of any kind has always been one of my favorite dishes to eat as well as to prepare. Using duck instead of beef or veal is a delicious variation that's easy and adds a special flair to the meal.

Tips to make it great:

> Use imported pasta (I like De Cecco bucatini #15).
>
> Do not overcook the pasta!

INGREDIENTS

5 duck legs

1/4 cup extra-virgin olive oil

1 garlic clove, minced

1/2 cup minced onion

1/2 cup minced carrot

1/4 cup minced celery

Himalayan pink salt, to taste

Black pepper, to taste

12 Niçoise olives, pitted and halved

1/2 cup dry red wine (I always use a wine I would drink rather than something labeled "cooking wine")

INSTRUCTIONS

1   If you can get your butcher to remove the skin from the duck legs, it will make your life much easier. If not, simply microwave the duck legs at high power for 1 minute, until warm, and the skin will come off much more easily.

2   After you've removed the skin, remove the meat from the bones. Cut the meat into bite-sized pieces and discard the bones.

3   In a deep and large frying pan, heat the olive oil. Add the garlic, onion, carrot, and celery, and season lightly with salt and pepper.

4   Cook over medium heat, stirring, until slightly softened, about 1 minute. Reduce the heat to low and cook, stirring, until browned, about 8 minutes.

(continued on next page)

INGREDIENTS (cont.)

2 cups chicken stock

6 tablespoons unsalted butter, divided

1 pound De Cecco bucatini pasta #15

1/2 cup freshly grated Parmigiano-Reggiano

INSTRUCTIONS (cont.)

5   Add the olives and sauté for about 1 minute. Add the duck and stir gently to coat with olive oil and mix with the vegetables. Add the wine and simmer for 1 minute. Add the chicken stock and simmer until the liquid has reduced to 3/4 cup, about 10 minutes. Remove from the heat and stir in half of the butter (3 tablespoons). Cover and keep warm.

6   In a large pot of boiling salted water, cook the bucatini until al dente and then drain. Add the cooked bucatini to the frying pan with your duck and sauce, and cook over moderate heat for 1 minute, stirring gently, until simmering.

7   Remove from the heat and stir in the cheese and the remaining 3 tablespoons of butter. Season with salt and pepper and serve.

ROAST DUCK AKA PEKING DUCK

Makes 4 servings

Prep Time: 15 minutes

Cook Time: 2 hours, plus 15 minutes to sit before carving

As you read in this chapter's introduction, this is a significant dish for me in respect to my numerous trips to China over the years. It's also very much rooted to my family, as we first discovered Peking Duck in New York's Chinatown in the 1980s. I've celebrated many birthdays over the years (either at home or dining out) enjoying Peking Duck. I find the flavor amazing, and I hope you do too.

Tips to make it great:

This recipe seems more complicated than it is, but still, try it on the weekend or when you have extra time. Expect a messy oven, and your smoke alarm might go off at some point. But it's worth it.

The best way to check if the duck is done is by using a meat thermometer. Insert the thermometer into the inner-thigh area near the breast. The duck is fully cooked when the temperature reaches 165 degrees F. If the duck isn't cooked yet but the skin is brown and crispy, loosely cover it with aluminum foil, and if using a convection oven, turn off the fan. The foil will prevent it from burning and allow you to continue cooking for a little longer.

Pair it with hoisin sauce, or for more authenticity, sweet bean sauce with cucumber and scallions.

(continued on next page)

INGREDIENTS

1 6- to 8-pound Peking duck, also known as Long Island duck

2 cups boiling water

1 tablespoon Himalayan pink salt

1 teaspoon black pepper

Hoisin sauce (optional for serving)

Mandarin pancakes (optional for serving)

Julienned scallions and cucumbers (optional for serving)

INSTRUCTIONS

1   Preheat the oven to 425 degrees F if using a convection oven or 390 degrees F if using a traditional oven. Make sure the rack you will cook the duck on is in the middle of the oven. You will likely need to remove one rack from your oven and reposition the other rack.

2   Rinse the duck and, if it was frozen, make sure that it is fully defrosted. Remove giblets from the cavity and trim any excess fat. Using the sharpest fork you have, prick the duck's skin all over.

3   Place a large roasting pan in the kitchen sink. Place a wire rack in the pan and set the duck on the wire rack so that it is suspended. Carefully pour boiling water all over both sides of the duck. This will tighten the skin and allow it to become super crispy in the oven.

4   Let the duck cool and dry completely. If you have time, I suggest you do the above steps one day in advance, leaving the duck in the refrigerator uncovered overnight.

5   Once the duck is at room temperature and dry, season it with salt and pepper. Place the duck breast side up on the wire rack in your roasting pan and roast it for 45 minutes.

6   Carefully turn the duck over. (I use two wooden spoons to do this.) Cook for an additional 45 minutes. Once again, turn the duck, now back to breast side up, and tilt it to allow any liquid (duck fat) to drip into the roasting pan. Roast for another 30 minutes.

7   Check the duck's internal temperature and make sure it is at 165 degrees F. By now, the duck should be golden brown, and its skin should be crispy. Remove the pan from the oven and place the duck on a large cutting board.

INSTRUCTIONS (cont.)

8   Let the duck rest for at least 15 to 20 minutes before you carve it, then carve just like you would a turkey, by removing the wings and drumsticks, and slicing the breast.

9   The only necessary accompaniment for this duck, from my perspective, is sauce. In Beijing, they serve duck of this style with *Tian Mian Jiang*, sweet bean sauce (even though it often doesn't have any beans) or sweet flour sauce. While I have enjoyed this sauce in Beijing, at home, I simply use hoisin sauce, which is thinner and soy-based. You can find it in the grocery store.

10 Serve the sliced duck with the sauce of your choice on thin Mandarin pancakes. You can purchase these at an Asian specialty market or online. I use Huntsy Peking Duck Wraps, made simply of flour and water. You can also add julienned scallions and cucumbers to the pancakes.

SAUTÉED MUSHROOMS WITH DUCK

Makes 4 to 6 servings

Prep Time: 15 minutes

Cook Time: 30 minutes

(15 minutes for duck separately and then about 15 for the vegetables)

Mushrooms are one of my all-time favorite side dishes. This recipe is full of flavor and can be enjoyed all year round.

Tips to make it great:

This is a great side dish that can be served warm or at room temperature.

The peppers take longer to cook than the onions and mushrooms.

INGREDIENTS

Cooking oil spray

2 duck breast halves (about 4 ounces each), skinned and boned

1/4 cup diced sweet red pepper

1/4 cup diced sweet yellow pepper

1/4 cup diced onion

10 mushrooms, sliced

1 teaspoon Himalayan pink salt

Red pepper flakes, to taste

INSTRUCTIONS

1 Preheat the oven to 450 degrees F.

2 Coat a large skillet with cooking oil spray. Place duck breasts into the oiled skillet and brown lightly over medium heat, approximately 1 to 3 minutes on each side.

3 Coat a baking dish with cooking oil spray, put the lightly browned duck into the baking dish, and bake for 20 minutes, or until done.

4 While the duck is cooking, dice the peppers and onions, and slice the mushrooms.

5 Once the duck is cooked, let it cool a bit before cutting it into bite-size pieces.

6 Using the same skillet you used to brown the duck, over medium heat, add the peppers first to soften them, then add the sliced mushrooms, and finally the onions. Once all the vegetables are almost fully cooked, add the duck pieces.

7 Add the salt and pepper flakes to taste.

ORANGE CREME BRULÉE WITH DUCK EGGS

Makes 4 servings

Total Prep Time: 45 minutes • Active Prep Time: 15 minutes

Cook Time: 45 minutes

This along with Zabaglione (page 184) is one of my mother-in-law's favorite desserts. It's a wonderful way to end a meal.

Tips to make it great:

> Use duck eggs! Because duck eggs contain more fat and protein and less water, and have a higher yolk/ white ratio than chicken eggs, they tend to produce fluffier cakes, higher meringues and souffles, and lighter breads and cookies. Ounce for ounce, duck eggs contain more Omega-3, Vitamins A and D, fatty acids, choline, folate, and iron than chicken eggs.

INGREDIENTS

2 cups heavy cream

1/4 cup granulated sugar, plus more for finishing and topping

Pinch Himalayan pink salt

Finely grated zest from 1/2 orange (about 1 tablespoon)

4 duck eggs (you'll only use the yolks)

INSTRUCTIONS

1 Preheat the oven to 325 degrees F.

2 Place 4 3/4-cup ramekins on a rimmed ovenproof pan deep enough to allow you to immerse the ramekins halfway in water before cooking.

3 In a saucepan over medium heat, combine the cream, sugar, and salt, stirring until the sugar dissolves and small bubbles appear around the edges of the cream, 4 to 5 minutes.

INSTRUCTIONS (cont.)

4   Remove from the heat and add the orange zest. Set at room temperature for at least 45 minutes. The longer the orange zest sits in the mixture, the more pronounced the flavor will be. Taste after 45 minutes and either allow it to infuse longer or strain the mixture through a fine-mesh sieve into a bowl.

5   Separate the yolks and whites of the eggs and place in separate bowls. You will only use the yolk and can save the white for an omelet or whatever else you want to make with them. Whisk the yolks until thickened, about 1 minute. Don't give up even if your arm starts to ache.

6   Gradually whisk the cooled sugary zest-cream mixture into the beaten yolks and strain through the fine-mesh sieve once more.

7   Move the ovenproof pan with the ramekins next to the oven.

8   Bring a pot of water to a boil, with enough water to fill the baking pan halfway up the sides of the ramekins.

9   Equally divide the custard between the 4 ramekins, then carefully transfer the pan with the custards into the oven.

10 Gently pour the hot water into the ovenproof dish, until the water reaches halfway up the sides of the ramekins. (You may recall this water-bath baking approach from my Cheesecake on page 32.) Bake until the custards are set but still move slightly in the center if shaken. This will take 20 to 35 minutes, so start checking at 5-minute intervals after 20 minutes.

11 Using tongs in one hand and a potholder in the other, carefully lift the custards out one at a time and place them on a wire rack. Let the custards cool on the rack for 25 minutes.

12 Wrap each with plastic wrap and refrigerate until well chilled, for 4 to 24 hours.

13 Right before you are ready to serve, sprinkle a thin layer of sugar on the top of each. Using a small kitchen torch, hold it over each ramekin and cook the thin layer of sugar until it caramelizes. Enjoy!

4

Throw Tomatoes

Bloody Mary with Jamón

Ischia Spritz

Pan Con Tomate

Not So Margherita Pizza

Sunday Gravy

Classic Tomato Salad

Tomatokeftedes

Red Snapper Livornese

Cherry Tomato Pops

Tomatoes, in one form or another, were at the heart of most meals I enjoyed growing up: as part of a sauce (no meat) or gravy (with meat), in a salad, or even simply eaten whole as a piece of fruit with a little salt. Many of my favorite recipes, as you'll discover, include tomatoes, which I also associate with many lessons in business and in life: about idiosyncrasies in the tax code, innovation, having a backup plan, decision-making, and time management.

It's hard for me to believe that until the 1700s, tomatoes were considered poisonous by many. It turns out that the European aristocracy ate from pewter plates, which happen to be high in lead. When tomatoes were served on the plates, the fruits' acidity caused the toxic lead from the plates to seep into the tomatoes, causing lead poisoning. The tomato was wrongly blamed, a reminder for me to always look for the root cause before coming to a conclusion.

The Italian city of Napoli and its amazing pizza are credited in part with changing the negative perception of tomatoes and allowing them to join the food mainstream. Folklore has it that Queen Margherita of Savoy, who was tired of eating French cuisine, requested something different from Chef Esposito of Pizzeria della Regina d'Italia. The queen enjoyed the pizza with tomato, cheese, and basil so much that it was named after her. This pizzeria in Napoli is now called Pizzeria Brandi, and if you visit it, you will find a plaque commemorating the Margherita pizza. (My fun take on this one is on page 58.)

You are likely aware that a tomato is classified botanically as a fruit. It is a seed-bearing product that grows from the ovary of a tomato plant, which means it is a fruit. Yet legally, a tomato is classified as a vegetable, as ruled by Supreme Court Justice Horace Gray in 1893. The reason for the tomato's reclassification was, of all things, tax revenue. The court noted that the tomatoes were scientifically fruits, but they classified them as a vegetable so that a 10-percent import tax on vegetables could be levied.

In the Supreme Court case, the Nix family, which imported tomatoes, was not pleased by the court's redrawing of scientific lines. The opinion seemed driven not by botany, but by the justices' experiences as diners. They wrote that vegetables were things "usually served at dinner in, with, or after the soup, fish, or meats . . . and not, like fruits generally, as dessert." Thus, the vegetable tax remained in place on a fruit.

High-quality inputs drive the success of most businesses. These inputs can be employees in service industries or raw materials in manufacturing settings. For example, a high-quality dress will be made from fabric that is tightly woven. Cooking is no different: quality in leads to quality out. One of the reasons the food in Italy is so spectacular is the quality of the vegetables and fruits—in particular, the tomatoes.

As an Italian American growing up on the East Coast in relatively small quarters, I don't recall jarring tomatoes. My grandmother cooked many dishes with tomatoes, but they mostly came from a can. Once the can was opened, often with injury from the sharp metal edges, the contents inside had to be strained and deseeded. Removing the seeds staved off their bitterness. My grandmother had a handheld metal food mill that slowly removed the seeds as she turned the handle. (I later made my children's baby food with that very food mill.)

Later in life, my grandmother introduced me to a company named Pomi, whose innovation replaced the need for both straining and deseeding. Pomi, a subsidiary of Parmalat, began importing strained tomatoes in boxes to the United States in 1982. Gone were the food mill and the cans! My grandmother's infatuation with the strained tomatoes in a box drove my infatuation with the company that produced them. Their innovative packaging was lighter and more sustainable: Forest Stewardship Council–certified packages made with paper from renewable forests.

When Pomi's parent company, Parmalat, hit hard times in the early 2000s—a long story of financial fraud—I was quite concerned about the future of Pomi tomatoes. Luckily, the subsidiary was bought in 2007 by Casalasco Società Agricola S.p.A, and Pomi is now part of the first supply chain in Italy for the farming and processing of tomatoes. Today, the company remains remarkably sustainable and has developed technology that allows consumers to track the location from which the tomatoes in each box are farmed.

As part of the brand's 40th anniversary, Pomi created a partnership with the government of New York City to fight hunger, donating more than 2,000 cartons of strained tomatoes to those in need. In my view, it remains a great example of a company that has solved a problem in an innovative, environmentally conscious way.

Thanks to Pomi and Queen Margherita and so many other examples, many of us think of Italy when we think of tomatoes. By no means does that country have a lock on this versatile fruit, though. Spain is another country I associate with tomatoes—and life lessons.

In 2009, I had the opportunity to visit Barcelona, Spain, for the first time. I attended a week-long seminar on entrepreneurship, coming away with new insight on timing the launch of a business and leading a new venture, among other topics. I also fell in love with the people, the food (in particular, *jamón ibérico* and *Pan Con Tomate,* page 57, and paella, page 174), and the architecture, including the works of Antoni Gaudí. I remembered Gaudí as a designer from studying architecture in high school, and I was keen on visiting Parque Güell and other structures and places he created.

As I learned about Gaudí as a person, I was quite inspired by his leadership. The building that gave me a greater understanding of him as a leader was his famous cathedral, La Sagrada Família. Gaudí and his financiers knew they would never see La Sagrada Família finished, yet his vision was so strong that he convinced multitudes of people to support him. He was confidently humble. Since my first visit to Barcelona, when someone tells me they have a compelling vision, I am always ready to listen. But first I remind them I have a high bar—a Gaudí bar.

Spain also gave me a vividly clear image of what I call the Tomato Test. As leaders, we are called to make tough decisions. Good leaders strive to ensure that their decision-making process is data-driven, transparent, and in the best interest of stakeholders. Those are important metrics for me, and I would add one more: whether a decision passes the Tomato Test. The test asks whether someone who learns about my decision would be angry or frustrated enough that they would want to throw tomatoes at me. It might not have an impact on the outcome of my decision, but it shapes the way in which I communicate it.

During the COVID-19 pandemic in 2020 and 2021, I communicated many decisions as a dean that failed the Tomato Test. Had the Gabelli School been teaching and learning entirely in person, I do think I would have been ducking tomatoes due to policies on wearing masks (or not) and developing high-flex courses (where some students are in the classroom and others are online). If the idea of throwing tomatoes intrigues you, consider attending La Tomatina, a festival in Buñol in Valencia, Spain, where attendees hurl more than 100 metric tons of tomatoes at each other on the last Wednesday of August every year.

I am blessed to have had a successful career as a professor and administrator, but tomatoes were at the center of a utopian idea I dreamed up for a career backup plan. When traveling through Italy, it is quite common to see local farmers selling tomatoes to people passing through their town. Our family would observe these farmers in various towns: some with sprawling, modernized farms, others with smaller and more modest farms, some young and others older, some men and some women, all with one thing in common: they appeared to possess deep joy. Perhaps it was the pride in their product or the peacefulness of the sea and the beauty of the land surrounding them.

My family members and I noticed the expressions on their faces and the contentment they appeared to convey. Over the years, as my husband and I would hit career snags or face what seemed like insurmountable challenges, we would declare, "I can always sell tomatoes in Italy." It was a backup plan that brought humor and levity to difficult situations. At one point in my career, when I found out I wasn't chosen for a role I was really interested in, I texted my family: "I am off to sell tomatoes." They knew immediately that I didn't get the job offer. Tomatoes remind me that having a backup plan, either real or utopian, is a healthy way to thrive in difficult times.

In my professional and personal life, I do my best to manage my time well. One technique that has helped me stems from the tomato theory of time management, better known as the Pomodoro Technique, developed by Francesco Cirillo in the late 1980s. Cirillo was a distracted university student who learned the value of using a timer (his was red and shaped like a tomato) to control his use of time and drive productivity. I regularly schedule my time in blocks and, when needed, set a "tomato" timer. Even in writing this book, I set aside blocks of time with ample timed breaks. By creating structure, time can be a great motivator. Good timing is essential for cooking as well. You can practice it when you try all of these tomato-inspired recipes.

BLOODY MARY WITH JAMÓN IBÉRICO

Makes 1 cocktail

Prep Time: 5 minutes

We serve this family twist on a traditional Bloody Mary often on Sundays in the summer as part of a late and leisurely brunch or early lunch. It's a delicious savory cocktail that we discovered while visiting and falling in love with Barcelona, Spain.

Tips to make it great:

> Have a lot of ice on hand and make sure all the ingredients are very cold.
>
> Have 3 glasses: 2 to mix with and 1 you will serve in.
>
> Serve in a chilled, tall 12-ounce glass.
>
> Garnish with a rolled slice of *jamón ibérico*, a pimento olive, and a lemon wedge on a toothpick.

INGREDIENTS

5 ounces tomato juice (you can also use V-8, which is milder, or Clamato, which has a clam flavor)

2 ounces vodka

1 teaspoon prepared horseradish

1 teaspoon Worcestershire sauce

1 teaspoon Tabasco sauce

Celery salt, to taste

Freshly ground black pepper, to taste

Lemon (to squeeze, plus a wedge for garnish)

1 slice of *jamón ibérico* (Spanish ham)

Two pimento olives

INSTRUCTIONS

1   Add the tomato juice, vodka, horseradish, Worcestershire, and Tabasco to a large glass, and add a sprinkle of celery salt, black pepper, and a squeeze of lemon.

2   Pour the contents of the glass into the second glass. Transfer the mixture back and forth 3 or 4 times.

3   Once all the ingredients are properly mixed, pour the mixture into the ice-filled serving glass.

4   Garnish as described in the "tips" section.

ISCHIA SPRITZ

Makes 1 cocktail

Prep Time: 5 minutes

On a recent trip to the island of Ischia, off the coast of Naples, Italy, I was introduced to this refreshing spritz. Mediterranean life in a glass!

Tips to make it great:

> Enjoy while watching the sunset in Ischia, or anywhere!
>
> Serve in a tall glass with plenty of ice.

INGREDIENTS

3 ounces Liquore al Pomodorino del Piennolo (if you can't find this liquor in your local shop, you can buy it online)

3 ounces Prosecco (I use La Marca)

1 piece of basil

Ice

INSTRUCTIONS

1   Fill a tall glass with ice. Add the Liquore al Pomodorino del Piennolo and then the Prosecco.

2   Place the basil leaf in the glass and serve.

PAN CON TOMATE

Makes 4 to 6 servings

Prep Time: 15 minutes • Cook Time: 15 minutes

This simple five-ingredient Spanish recipe is an absolute favorite of both my daughters, but it took a bit of trial and error for me to get it right. The first time I prepared it, the tomatoes weren't ripe enough, so choose the best, juiciest, and ripest tomatoes for this. It makes a huge difference.

Tips to make it great:

> Use fresh semolina bread.
>
> Use ripe, juicy tomatoes, and use salt generously.

INGREDIENTS

1 loaf of seeded semolina bread (you also can use ciabatta)

1/4 cup extra-virgin olive oil, divided

2 or 3 peeled cloves of fresh garlic

2 large ripe tomatoes

3 slices of _jamón ibérico_ (optional)

1 tablespoon Himalayan pink salt

Black pepper, to taste

INSTRUCTIONS

1 Preheat the oven to 300 degrees F.

2 Slice the semolina bread from the top down the middle so you have two long pieces of bread. Now slice the bread into 1 1/2-inch pieces. You should end up with about 14 to 16 pieces of bread.

3 Using a pastry brush, generously brush the bread with 2 tablespoons of the olive oil. Rub each piece of bread with the garlic cloves. Place the bread on a baking sheet and bake until light brown and crispy, about 15 minutes.

(continued on next page)

INSTRUCTIONS (cont.)

4   Meanwhile, halve the tomatoes and grate them using a large cheese grater or box grater into a large bowl (watch your fingers!). The skin of the tomatoes will be left in your hands and can be discarded.

5   Season the grated tomatoes with salt and pepper, and add the remaining 2 tablespoons of olive oil.

6   Spoon the tomato mixture over bread. Serve immediately.

7   For an added delight, place a slice of *jamón ibérico* on top.

NOT SO MARGHERITA PIZZA

Makes 4 to 6 servings

Prep Time: 15 minutes

Cook Time: 15 minutes in two segments

This fun and simple recipe is a playful variation on the classic Margherita pizza that I wrote about in the chapter introduction. This recipe brings back so many great memories. I'm guessing that I made these *hundreds* of times when my children were growing up. Now I enjoy making them for my grandchildren. Adults love my English muffin pizzas too. I can never make enough!

Tips to make it great:

Be creative and add different toppings—anything from artichoke hearts to arugula. Use different cheeses as well. Mozzarella and goat cheese are great alternatives to muenster.

Let the children in your life help. This was one of the first dishes our children learned how to prepare.

INGREDIENTS

2 packages of English muffins (I like Thomas' English Muffins)

Extra-virgin olive oil, for oiling the muffins

12 ounces marinara sauce (either prepare your own using the recipe on page 190 or use jarred—I've used Lidia's Marinara with great success when pressed for time)

1/2 cup grated Parmigiano-Reggiano

12 slices muenster cheese

1 cup oil-cured black olives (optional)

12 anchovy filets (optional)

INSTRUCTIONS

1 Preheat the oven to 400 degrees F.

2 Line a baking sheet with parchment paper or aluminum foil and place the English muffins on it. Bake for 5 minutes, until the muffins are lightly toasted.

3 Remove from the oven and lightly drizzle them with olive oil. You may want to use a pastry brush.

4 Spoon each muffin half evenly with the prepared tomato sauce. Sprinkle each evenly with Parmigiano-Reggiano. Top each with one slice of muenster cheese and whatever toppings you like. In our house, oil-cured black olives and anchovies were often favorites.

5 Bake for 7 to 8 minutes, until the cheese is melted, and let cool before serving. You'll be surprised how many muffins people can eat, so keep extra on hand.

SUNDAY GRAVY WITH MEATBALLS

Makes 4 to 6 servings

Prep Time: 30 minutes

Cook Time: 3 hours + 10 minutes

This super-comforting, meaty red sauce is a staple at just about every holiday. Because of that, it's also the first recipe I shared with my community of colleagues at the Gabelli School of Business. When I did so, it kicked off an annual tradition. At any time of year, you can open my freezer and find a few containers of my Sunday Gravy ready to be defrosted on demand. It's that good. I hope you love it as much as my family, colleagues, and students do.

Tips to make it great:

Use bone-in meat.

Use Pomi tomatoes and serve with ricotta and Parmigiano-Reggiano.

Be sure to cook the pasta al dente.

Throw Tomatoes

For Gravy

INGREDIENTS

Extra-virgin olive oil

1 pound piece of beef, ideally bone-in

1 pound piece of veal, ideally bone-in

4 pork spareribs (you can substitute beef spareribs)

4 links sweet sausage

3 peeled garlic cloves, chopped

4 26-ounce boxes Pomi strained tomatoes

1/2 cup chopped parsley

Himalayan pink salt and pepper, to taste

INSTRUCTIONS

1   Glaze the bottom of a frying pan with olive oil and over medium-high heat brown the beef, veal, spareribs, and sausage (I usually halve them). Once browned, place in a bowl and set side.

2   Glaze the bottom of a large saucepan with olive oil, and over medium heat add the garlic and cook, stirring occasionally, until lightly brown.

3   Pour in the 4 boxes of tomatoes. Fill one empty box a quarter of the way with water, and then pour that water into other empty boxes in order to get all remaining tomatoes out of the boxes and into the pan.

4   Add the entire pan of pre-browned meat, parsley, salt, and pepper to the saucepan, and stir with a wooden spoon. Bring the gravy to a boil and leave the spoon in the pot. Once the gravy boils for a minute, lower the heat and simmer for 3 hours.

(continued on next page)

For Meatballs

INGREDIENTS

1 1/2 pounds of ground pork/beef/veal mixture (you can substitute ground turkey)

2 tablespoons ricotta

1/2 cup seasoned breadcrumbs (can also use whole wheat)

1/2 cup whole milk

3 extra large eggs

Himalayan pink salt and pepper, to taste

Extra-virgin olive oil, for frying

INSTRUCTIONS

Note: The longer the meatballs sit in the gravy, the more well cooked they will become.

1 Mix all of the meatball ingredients together, except for the olive oil, until you no longer see traces of any egg, and everything is evenly distributed.

2 Form the mixture into small meatballs (you want about 25).

3 Pour olive oil into a frying pan until it is a quarter of the way filled. Heat the oil over medium-high heat until it is almost sizzling. I usually drop some breadcrumbs to see if it is hot enough.

4 Once the oil is hot enough, put the meatballs into the oil one at a time (using a spoon to do so is easiest for me) until the pan is fairly full. You might need to do this in batches.

5 Cook the meatballs until one side is lightly browned, then turn them and continue to cook until all sides are lightly browned. Remove the meatballs from the pan and place on a paper towel-lined tray. Once the meatballs have cooled, drop them into the gravy. (Note: if you want a healthier approach, you can also bake the meatballs on a baking sheet.)

For Pasta and Serving

———

INGREDIENTS

1 or 2 1-pound boxes of De Cecco mezze rigatoni #26 or other pasta

1/4 cup of iodized salt for boiling water

Ricotta, for serving

Parmigiano-Reggiano, for serving

INSTRUCTIONS

1   When you are ready to prepare the pasta, boil a large pot of water and, once boiling, add a 1/4 cup of iodized salt. Cook the pasta to al dente. Drain and serve topped with ricotta and Parmigiano.

2   Note that 1 pound of pasta is usually ample for 4 people, if you are serving it with some side dishes. This recipe makes enough gravy for at least 1 pound of pasta, so you can either keep half for leftovers, or invite 4 more people over.

CLASSIC TOMATO SALAD

Makes 4 to 6 servings

Prep Time: 15 minutes

I am still not sure if the best tomatoes I've ever eaten were in Italy or in Greece. There is something about the rich soil in both countries that unfortunately just cannot be replicated in the United States, though I must admit, Hamptons tomatoes and Amish tomatoes are also quite delicious. This recipe is a combination of my favorite parts of both the Greek and Italian tomato salads that I especially enjoy.

Tips to make it great:

> Make sure you have ripe and juicy tomatoes.
>
> All ingredients should be at room temperature, especially the tomatoes.
>
> Replace the feta cheese with shaved Parmigiano-Reggiano for an equally delicious variation.

INGREDIENTS

4 large heirloom tomatoes

3 tablespoons extra-virgin olive oil, divided

1/2 cup Kalamata olives

1/4 cup crumbled feta cheese or 1/4 cup shaved Parmigiano-Reggiano

1/2 teaspoon black pepper

1 teaspoon Himalayan pink salt

1 tablespoon balsamic vinegar

INSTRUCTIONS

1   Slice the tomatoes into 6 to 8 wedges and place them in a large bowl. Pour 2 tablespoons of the olive oil over them, salt them, and set aside for 5 minutes.

2   Add the crumbled feta or shaved Parmigiano-Reggiano, black pepper, the remaining tablespoon of olive oil and the balsamic vinegar, then stir in the olives. Serve at room temperature.

TOMATOKEFTEDES

Serves 4 to 6

Prep Time: 15 minutes • Cook Time: 5 minutes

The first time I made these tomato pancakes, which are plump and almost like savory fritters, was during a cooking class I took in Santorini, Greece. The tomatoes were extraordinary. But even with supermarket tomatoes, this recipe is wonderful!

Tips to make it great:

> Use ripe, juicy tomatoes.
>
> Serve immediately.

INGREDIENTS

4 ripe tomatoes

1 onion, diced

1/2 bunch of spearmint, finely chopped

1 cup Kefalotyri grated cheese (this is a Greek cheese made from goat milk; you may be able to find it at a specialty market, and if not, you can use Pecorino Romano)

1 extra large egg

Himalayan pink salt, to taste

Black pepper, to taste

1/4 cup, plus 1 tablespoon flour

3 tablespoons extra-virgin olive oil for frying

INSTRUCTIONS

1   Wash the tomatoes and chop them finely. You can use a cheese grater if you prefer. Either way, put them in a colander to drain any excess liquid. Place the drained tomatoes in a large bowl along with the onion and mix well.

2   Add the mint, cheese, egg, salt, and pepper. Stir to combine and then gradually add the flour. The resulting mixture should be wet but should have some consistency. If it is too wet, add a little more flour.

3   In a large skillet, heat the oil over medium-high heat. Once the oil is heated, take a tablespoon and fill it up with the mixture. Slip the mixture into the oil, being careful not to burn your hand. Fry each pancake for 2 minutes on each side.

4   Place the finished tomato pancakes on a paper towel–lined platter to drain excess oil and serve hot.

RED SNAPPER LIVORNESE

Makes 4 to 6 servings

Prep Time: 15 minutes • Cook Time: 20 minutes

I decided to learn how to make this dish for my father after he ordered it in a local restaurant and was disappointed in the quality of the fish. Over the years, it became one of his all-time favorite dishes. It's quick and easy to make and loaded with color and flavor. I think it's as pleasing to the eyes as it is to the palate.

Tips to make it great:

Make sure the fish is fresh.

Use white wine you would drink rather than cooking wine.

Make extra sauce and serve with rice or pasta.

INGREDIENTS

2 tablespoons extra-virgin olive oil

1 onion, diced

12 black cured olives, pitted and chopped

2 tablespoons capers

4 red snapper filets (be sure that all of the bones are out by running your fingers over the areas where the bones were)

2 cups Lidia's or Pomi marinara sauce, or make your own marinara sauce (see page 190)

1 cup white wine

Himalayan pink salt and pepper to taste (note: olives are salty, so be careful not to overdo the salt)

INSTRUCTIONS

1   Preheat the oven to 350 degrees F.

2   Heat olive oil in a large skillet you can use both on top of the stove and in the oven. A Le Creuset sauté pan is perfect. If your sauté pan isn't large enough to hold all four pieces of fish, you will need to use two pans.

3   Add onion to the heated olive oil and cook until it gets soft, around 4 minutes. Add the olives and cook for another 3 minutes. Lay the snapper skin-side down in the pan and pour the wine and tomato sauce on top of the fish. Once all ingredients are in the pan, remove the pan from the stovetop and place it in the oven for 15 minutes.

CHERRY TOMATO POPS

Makes 4 to 6 servings

Prep Time: 15 minutes • Cook Time: 10 minutes

I often creatively substituted cherry tomatoes for candy as a treat and a dessert for my kids while they were growing up. This recipe went a long way in helping me to convince them that certain fruits and veggies are maybe just sweets in a different outfit. Now I'm on a mission to convince my grandchildren that cherry tomatoes are a treat and can be as satisfying as candy. It's mostly working.

Tips to make it great:

Be ready to serve immediately.

Experiment with different toppings, such as chocolate.

INGREDIENTS

16 cherry tomatoes

1/3 cup sesame seeds or sprinkles, for coating the tomatoes

15 Werther's Original Chewy Caramels

2 tablespoons heavy cream

INSTRUCTIONS

1   Place each cherry tomato onto a wooden skewer.

2   Ready a small bowl of sesame seeds or sprinkles to dip the caramel tomatoes in.

3   Using a double boiler (water in the bottom pot and an empty pot on top), put the unwrapped caramels into the top pot and add the heavy cream. Boil the water until the caramel is melted.

4   As soon as the caramel is melted, work quickly to dip each tomato into the caramel to fully coat, and then immediately dip the tomato into the bowl with the seeds or sprinkles. Set on a baking sheet.

5   Continue until all tomatoes are dipped. Serve immediately.

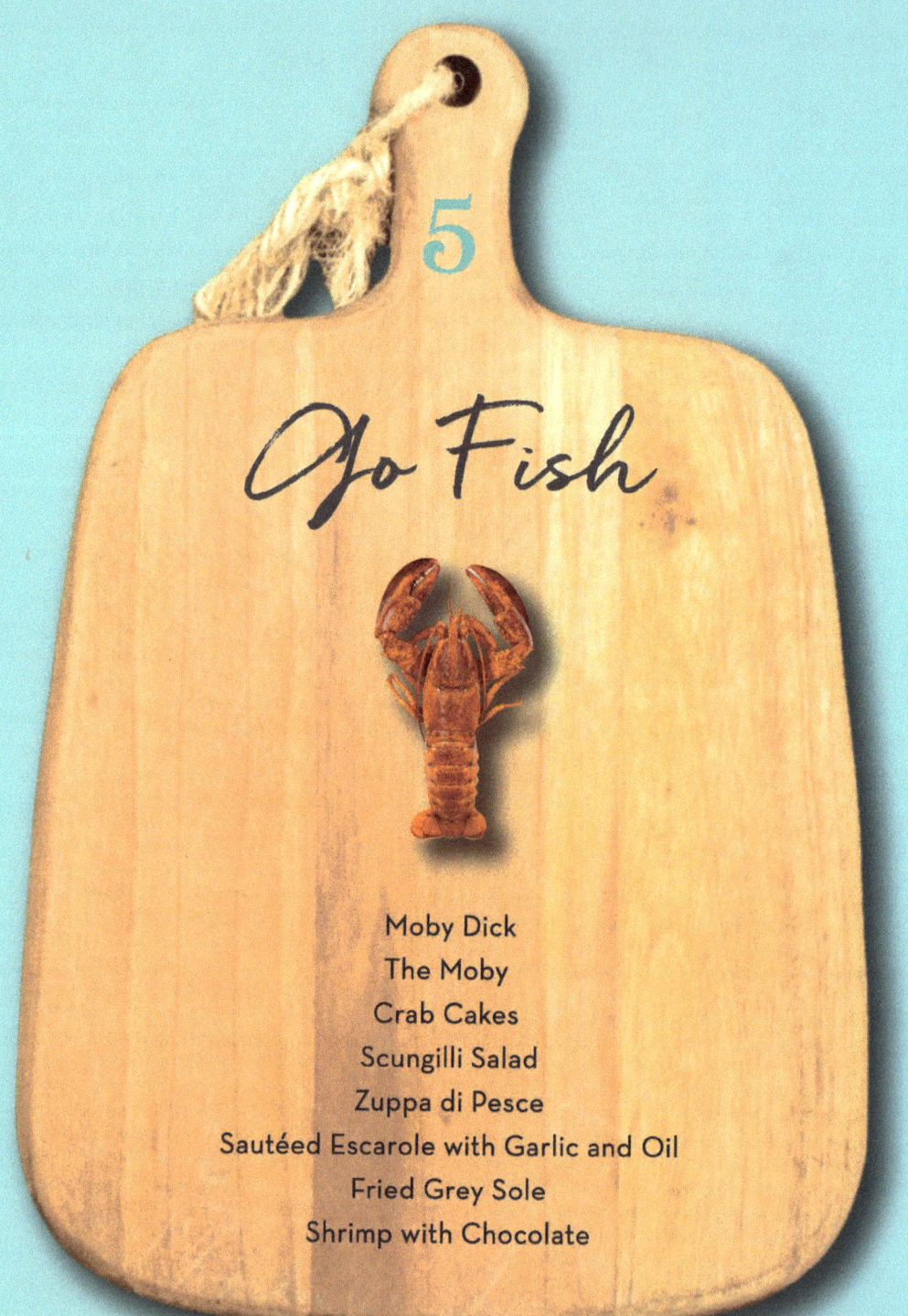

5

Go Fish

Moby Dick
The Moby
Crab Cakes
Scungilli Salad
Zuppa di Pesce
Sautéed Escarole with Garlic and Oil
Fried Grey Sole
Shrimp with Chocolate

The adage "Give a man a fish, and you feed him for a day; teach a man to fish, and you feed him for a lifetime" has always resonated with me. Perhaps it's one of the reasons I became a professor. I am, after all, a teacher at heart, always trying to show and explain. I prefer to let someone try on their own rather than doing it for them, though. The chapter on fish calls forth a few memories and lessons, including how to be a good sport and the importance of humor, authenticity, and risk-taking.

As a kid, I played a few card games, among them 500 Rummy and poker, but one of the first I remember playing is Go Fish. As you probably remember, it's a matching game. You ask another player if they are holding a certain card. If they are, they must give it to you, and then you play that pair. If they aren't, they tell you to "go fish," requiring you to draw a card and increase the numbers of cards you're holding. The game taught me about numbers, patterns, and strategy, and it also enhanced my memory.

My most important takeaway from Go Fish, however, was how to be a good sport and win graciously. In my family, being a good sport was not a natural instinct: the words "go fish" were often said a bit vengefully. As someone who was often "sent fishing," I knew the sinking feeling of picking up card after card, looking desperately for a match. As a result, when I sent an opponent fishing, I tried to do so with an empathetic smile. That empathy and innate sense that "what goes around comes around" has guided me through all sorts of personal and professional situations. While I wholeheartedly enjoy winning, I don't enjoy others losing.

Outside of our card games, my family ate a good amount of fish—primarily shellfish. We often dined on shrimp, crab, scungilli, calamari, and snails. One family snail dish involved tomato sauce. We called it Babbalucci, Sicilian slang for "snail." My grandmother would buy the snails at the fish store and put them in a tightly covered pot to soak before cooking them. There were a few occasions when the pot was not covered properly, and the snails escaped and discovered a new world inside the refrigerator! My grandmother would collect the escapees with a sense of humor and respect for their tenacity. Her response was a wonderful lesson in not taking yourself too seriously, and it was another example of what to do when "life hands you lemons." This time, make Babbalucci!

When I became a mother myself, I discovered that trying new foods—snails in particular—helped our children practice taking risks in a controlled setting. Given my sentiment about chicken (see chapter 8), it's ironic that any time we wanted to get our children to take a risk on a new food—venison, frog legs and the like—we would tell them it was chicken.

The most outlandish example of "Try it, it's chicken" was snails prepared escargot style with garlic and butter. I had grown accustomed to snails as a child, with my mom and grandmother both preparing them for us. My mom even had her own reusable snail shells and special utensils to hold the shell while you searched for the snail. In restaurants we would order escargot and thoroughly enjoy the dish, soaking up the butter and garlic. Our children, however, didn't know that escargot was snails until they were much older. By then, they had developed such a taste for them that it didn't matter. Experimenting with food became a great way for them to take small risks that reaped delicious rewards.

As you realize by now, my dad was a very fun-loving guy. He made a joke about just about everything. When he was in his 40s, he quit smoking and steadily began gaining weight. In the 1980s, just like today, there were many fad diets. When someone would mention the latest diet they were trying, my dad would respond, "I am on a seafood diet. I see food, and I eat it." No matter how many times he said it, he would get a laugh. He really didn't care what people thought. It was an amazing gift he had, the ability to be himself no matter what the setting. I must admit I sometimes saw his authenticity as a bit over the top, but as my leadership responsibilities evolved, the importance of humor and being myself became central to my leadership style.

As a Bronx girl, my diction and mannerisms proudly advertise my hometown. Early in my career, I would beat myself up when I butchered a word or phrase, but over time I realized I should give myself a little grace. Much of the time no one but me even noticed the mispronunciation. I also learned that humor eases most situations. In fact, while I served as dean, I tried to infuse lightheartedness into tense or challenging situations by sharing a story or anecdote.

When the university asked my division to provide additional revenue to support those who were underperforming, I'd say, "I'm happy to contribute to the party. I'll bring the shrimp cocktail, or even the lobster tails, but I can't bring the whole meal." It always got a smile and made the point.

I only cooked a whole lobster once, so I won't share a recipe for that, but I will share a story. I remember being very excited about making a lobster dinner. I got a new pot large enough to steam several lobsters and bought lobster bibs and claw crackers. In the Little Italy area of the Bronx, there remains a wonderful fish store, Randazzo's Fish Market. I went there to pick up my live lobsters, their claws clapped shut with a rubber band.

At home in my kitchen, I had the pot ready, but just as I was about to put the first live lobster into the pot, I felt absolutely awful. The fact that I was killing a living crustacean hit me like a ton of bricks. Though I completed the deadly task, I was unable to eat the lobster I had prepared. Everyone else enjoyed "the sweetest lobster they ever ate." It took me a few years to eat a whole lobster again, and now it is only when I am out to dinner. While I have enjoyed lobster in Maine and the Caribbean, my favorite is from Gosman's Dock restaurant in Montauk.

When Fordham University designed its new business school space at Lincoln Center, we repurposed an older building that required us to creatively use interior space. Part of the design included a small glass-enclosed classroom in the middle of the floor plan, surrounded by hallways and faculty offices. The glass was expensive, but I believed it would allow light in and create a more interesting learning space than a fully drywalled room. On completion, it was affectionately named the fishbowl. I found it wonderful to look in and see our students engaged.

Over time, the faculty members who taught in the fishbowl said students were distracted by things happening outside the room, and they asked if we could add an appliqué to the glass. I reluctantly agreed, but I requested that as much of the glass as possible remain transparent. I assumed the appliqué would go no higher than eye level of a person seated inside the classroom. But I should have remembered what Felix Unger, played by Tony Randall, taught us about what happens when you assume: "You make an ass out of 'u' and 'me.'" Once the appliqué was in place, the only visibility into the fishbowl was through a tiny border close to the ceiling. The students and faculty who used the room were happy, but I was frustrated at the lack of transparency and the wasted investment. My main takeaway from that experience was, make sure you ask. If I had asked a few pre-installation questions, we could have covered some of the glass and not all of it.

In my kitchen over the years, I have often cooked Fried Grey Sole (page 80, a favorite of all three of my children) and Red Snapper Livornese (page 66), but I got the most satisfaction out of cooking shellfish. For many years, I made a wonderful Zuppa di Pesce (page 77) with a crab base. Inspired by a local restaurant's scungilli salad recipe, I made some adjustments (page 76), leading to rave reviews from my diners. You'll find all of these recipes, and more, in this chapter.

I have only been fishing a handful of times, always from a boat. Each time, I realized the importance of patience. There is a lot of waiting, keeping an eye out for change, and being ready to try a new spot. Some of the recipes in this chapter will require you to be patient, but they are likely to get you out of your comfort zone and help you try new things. Buon appetito!

MOBY DICK

Makes 1 cocktail

Prep Time: 5 minutes

Sit down with a copy of Herman Melville's classic 400-plus-page novel, *Moby Dick*, and enjoy this cocktail with the same name! In addition to inspiring this drink (and its cousin, the Moby, on the following page), the novel is the source of the name of one of America's behemoth coffee chains. Starbucks is named after Captain Ahab's first mate, Starbuck, who served on the Pequod. This drink will fill you with a bit of adventure and maybe even transport you to the high seas.

Tips to make it great:

Use Zacapa dark rum along with Angostura bitters, imported from Trinidad and Tobago and made by the oldest manufacturer of bitters.

Be sure to use plenty of ice and chill tall glasses in advance.

INGREDIENTS

2 ounces dark rum

1/2 ounces lime juice, and a slice of lime for garnish

2 dashes bitters

3 ounces ginger beer, regular or diet

INSTRUCTIONS

1   Put four large ice cubes into a chilled tall glass. Pour in the rum, then squeeze in the lime juice and add the bitters.

2   Top off with the ginger beer, and garnish with a slice of lime.

THE MOBY

Makes 1 cocktail

Prep Time: 5 minutes

I tweaked this cocktail ever so slightly from a recipe in Tim Federle's book, *Tequila Mockingbird: Cocktails with a Literary Twist.*

Tips to make it great:

Use crushed ice.

Use Grey Goose vodka.

INGREDIENTS

1/2 cup crushed ice

2 ounces vodka

1 ounce Blue Curaçao

1 ounce of club soda or, for a sweeter taste, Sprite

1 Swedish Fish gummy, for garnish

INSTRUCTIONS

1   Fill a shaker with the crushed ice. Pour the vodka and Blue Curaçao into it. Shake well.

2   Pour into a chilled martini glass, then add the club soda or Sprite.

3   Garnish with a Swedish Fish on a toothpick.

CRAB CAKES

Makes 5 to 6 servings as an appetizer (yields 10 mini crab cakes)
Prep Time: 15 minutes • Cook Time: 10 minutes

Crab cakes are a summertime favorite—easy to prepare and easy to enjoy with a drink if you make them bite-sized. After reading this recipe, however, my daughter Diana may never eat my crab cakes again. She has an aversion to mayonnaise, and I never shared with her (until now!) that the reason my crab cakes are so good is not just the high-quality crab, but also the mayonnaise.

Tips to make it great:

> Use high-quality, fresh lump crab meat.
>
> Omit the Old Bay seasoning that many recipes call for.

INGREDIENTS

2 tablespoons extra-virgin olive oil

1/4 cup chopped red bell pepper

1/4 cup chopped onions

16 ounces lump crabmeat, drained

2 extra large eggs

2 tablespoons mayonnaise

1 teaspoon dry mustard

1 teaspoon garlic powder

1/2 teaspoon Himalayan pink salt

1/2 teaspoon ground black pepper

INSTRUCTIONS

1   Add 2 tablespoons of olive oil to a skillet and sauté the red pepper and onions over medium heat briefly until tender. Set aside to cool.

2   In a large bowl, combine the crabmeat, sautéed red peppers and onion, eggs, mayonnaise, dry mustard, garlic powder, salt, and pepper. Mix well but don't overmix, as you want the crab meat to partly remain in lumps. Form the mixture into small balls, about a 1/2-inch wide.

INGREDIENTS (cont.)

1/2 cup panko breadcrumbs

1/2 cup seasoned breadcrumbs

1/4 cup extra-virgin olive oil, or as needed

INSTRUCTIONS (cont.)

3 In a large flat dish, combine the panko and seasoned breadcrumbs. Roll the crab balls in the breadcrumbs until they are mostly covered, erring on the side of less rather than more. (You don't want the breading to overpower the crab cake.) Once the balls are mostly covered in breadcrumbs, flatten them gently so that they resemble small sliders.

4 Heat the olive oil in a large skillet over medium-high heat. Cook the cakes until they are golden brown on each side. This should take 1 to 2 minutes per side. Place on a paper towel–lined plate and serve immediately.

If you want a quick and tasty dipping sauce, mix this together in a large bowl:

2/3 cup of mayonnaise

2 tablespoons lemon juice

1 tablespoon Dijon mustard

1 teaspoon Worcestershire sauce

1/2 teaspoon paprika

1/2 teaspoon cayenne pepper

SCUNGILLI SALAD

Makes 6 to 8 servings • Prep Time: 15 minutes

Scungilli is sea conch, and it's not easy to find it fresh in New York City. As a result, I use canned San LaMonica scungilli. This recipe is a variation of the scungilli salad served at a local Bronx restaurant called The Williamsbridge Inn. This salad is a family favorite.

Tips to make it great:

Make it a day in advance to allow the scungilli to marinate.

Use high-quality extra-virgin olive oil.

INGREDIENTS

1 29-ounce can scungilli, rinsed well and drained

1/4 cup finely chopped red onion

2 tablespoons capers

1/2 cup black pearl olives, quartered

1/4 cup finely chopped roasted red bell peppers

3 tablespoons extra-virgin olive oil

2 tablespoons red wine vinegar

2 lemons, divided

1/4 bunch of fresh parsley, chopped

1/4 teaspoon Himalayan pink salt

1/2 teaspoon pepper

1/2 head of iceberg lettuce

INSTRUCTIONS

1   As noted above, thoroughly rinse the scungilli. Use a colander. Make sure the foam and strong smell have disappeared. Dry the scungilli with a paper towel and set aside.

2   In a large bowl, add the onions, capers, olives, and roasted peppers and stir to combine. Add the scungilli and continue stirring. Add the olive oil and vinegar and squeeze 1 lemon into the bowl. Add the parsley, salt, and pepper and stir to incorporate.

3   Cover with plastic wrap and refrigerate for at least 1 hour. If you are able to leave it overnight, it will taste even better. When you are ready to serve it, chop up the iceberg lettuce and put it into the bowl with all the other ingredients. Squeeze the remaining lemon on top and stir to incorporate.

ZUPPA DI PESCE

Makes 6 to 8 servings

Prep time: 15 minutes • Cook time: 2 hours

I always make this seafood-loaded soup on Christmas Eve, and I also make it at least once a summer. It's one of my husband's solid-gold favorites. He has a hard time not ordering it when we eat out if it's on the menu. He's enjoyed Zuppa di Pesce all over the world, and at some of New York City's finest restaurants. His absolute favorite (other than mine!) is at Baby Moon, a family-style restaurant in Westhampton on the east end of Long Island.

Tips to make it great:

Serve over escarole or black (squid ink) pasta.

Do not overcook the shellfish.

INGREDIENTS

1 pound black mussels

1 pound baby Manila clams

1/4 cup extra-virgin olive oil

1 onion, diced

1 large leek, halved lengthwise and thinly sliced

Himalayan pink salt, to taste

1 teaspoon red pepper flakes (optional)

2 8-ounce bottles clam juice

2 pounds lump crab meat from a plastic container (preferable to a can)

3 26-ounce boxes Pomi tomatoes

INSTRUCTIONS

1   Wash the mussels and clams and immerse in a pot of cold water for 30 minutes. Empty the water, scrub the clams and mussels again, and let them sit for another 30 minutes. By the end of the second 30 minutes, the shells should all still be closed. If any are open, discard them.

2   In a very large cast-iron or stainless steel pot, heat the olive oil and sauté the garlic, onion, and leek with a pinch of salt and a pinch of pepper until translucent. Add the red pepper flakes if you like and clam juice, making sure to scrape all the brown bits from the bottom. Simmer until reduced by half. Add the lump crab meat and stir until thoroughly incorporated.

(continued on next page)

INGREDIENTS (cont.)

1 pound calamari (mixed circles and tentacles)

4 lobster tails

2 pounds jumbo shrimp, cleaned and peeled with tails on

6 cloves of garlic, minced

1/2 cup fresh parsley, chopped

Black pepper to taste

INSTRUCTIONS (cont.)

3   Add the tomatoes and parsley to the pot and simmer over very low heat for 30 minutes. Add the calamari and let simmer for 1 additional hour.

4   Add all the clams and mussels to the pot together with the lobster tails and simmer uncovered for about 10 minutes until all the clams and mussels have opened and the lobster shells have turned bright red. Last, add the shrimp and cook for another 10 minutes. Discard any clams or mussels that haven't opened.

Note: If you plan on serving pasta, about 30 minutes before your Zuppa is complete, bring a separate pot filled with water to a boil. I have used store-bought black pasta or prepared my own (see page 182). Once the pasta is ready, strain well and pour the sauce over it. This recipe also can be served over a bed of sautéed escarole. See recipe on the following page for how to prepare the escarole.

SAUTÉED ESCAROLE WITH GARLIC AND OIL

Makes 4 to 6 servings

Prep Time: 5 minutes active, and 15 minutes to soak the escarole

Cook Time: 5 minutes

You can serve this as a side dish or as a substitute for pasta if you like. You can also add a can of cannellini beans and some chicken broth to magically transform it into an easy soup.

INGREDIENTS

2 heads of escarole

3 tablespoons extra-virgin olive oil

1 garlic clove, minced

1/2 teaspoon Himalayan pink salt

INSTRUCTIONS

1   Cut the head off the escarole and cut up each leaf into about 3 pieces. Rinse the escarole in a colander and then place it in a very large pot of cold water for about 15 minutes.

2   Drain the escarole over the colander and make sure any dirt is washed away. Pat dry with a paper towel.

3   In a large sauté pan over medium heat, heat the oil and then add the garlic. Once the garlic starts to brown, add the escarole leaves a bunch at a time. Cook quickly in about 2 minutes. Remove and add the next batch. The water may splatter, so be careful. Add a little of the salt to each batch.

FRIED GREY SOLE

Makes 4 to 6 servings

Prep Time: 5 minutes • Cook Time: 10 minutes

Fried grey sole is yet another family favorite. When the kids were little, I often served it on Friday night during Lent alongside macaroni and cheese. My son James loves it so much that he still asks me to make this as part of his birthday dinner.

Tips to make it great:

> Do not overcook!
>
> Squeeze lemon on the fish just before serving.

INGREDIENTS

2 large eggs

1/4 cup whole milk

3/4 cup 4C Seasoned Bread Crumbs or any brand you choose

1/4 teaspoon black pepper

6 (8-ounce) grey sole filets

1/4 cup extra-virgin olive oil

1 lemon, for juice and for garnish

INSTRUCTIONS

1 Beat the eggs in a shallow bowl and mix in the milk.

2 In a flat dish, combine the bread crumbs and black pepper. Fully submerge a filet in the egg mixture, and then place it on the plate with the breadcrumbs, fully covering both sides of the fish. Repeat this with all of the filets.

3 Once all of the fish is breaded, heat the olive oil in a large nonstick frying pan over medium-high heat. Be sure that the oil is hot enough: drop some breadcrumbs into the oil and check to see that they sizzle.

INSTRUCTIONS (cont.)

4   Put the filets in the pan and cook, turning once, until golden brown, about 2 minutes on each side. You might have to do this in batches. Remove the lightly browned filets and place them on a paper towel-lined platter to drain any excess oil.

5   Right before serving, squeeze the fresh lemon juice over the fish. It's best to serve immediately, but I've enjoyed many fish sandwiches the next day.

SHRIMP WITH CHOCOLATE

Makes 4 to 6 servings

Prep Time: 15 minutes • Cook Time: 20 minutes

Looking for something fun and different? Try the lobster ice cream at Ben & Bill's Chocolate Emporium in downtown Bar Harbor, Maine. That's their recipe. Here you get my own adventurous alternative: shrimp with chocolate.

INGREDIENTS

1 cup high-quality dark chocolate (at least 70% cacao), chopped

1/2 cup whole milk

3 tablespoons extra-virgin olive oil

2 cloves garlic, crushed

1 pound shrimp, peeled and deveined (12- to 14-count)

Dash of Himalayan pink salt

1 cup white wine (not cooking wine)

1/4 cup chopped parsley

INSTRUCTIONS

1   Set up a double boiler or a stainless-steel bowl on top of a small pot of boiling water (just make sure that the bottom of the bowl is not touching the water).

2   In the top part of the double boiler or in the stainless-steel bowl, combine the chopped chocolate and the milk. Stir the mixture using a rubber spatula until the chocolate is completely melted and the mixture is smooth.

3   In a large sauté or frying pan, heat the olive oil and sauté the garlic until soft. Add the shrimp and cook until the shrimp is pink. Add the salt and wine, and let the wine reduce. Then add the parsley. Transfer the shrimp to a flat plate. Drizzle the shrimp with the melted chocolate and serve immediately.

6

What's Up, Doc?

Spiked Carrot Juice (or Not)

Air-Fried Carrot Chips

Spaghetti Primavera

Carrot Fagioli Sliders

Miso Butter Carrots

Carrot Cake

Carrots have always conjured positive sentiments for me. Perhaps it is the high level of vitamin A, the antitoxins, the beta-carotene, my fondness for Bugs Bunny, or the fact that in English, a carrot has become a metaphor for something good. In addition to providing positive feelings, carrots have shined a light on influence, decision-making, leadership, gratitude, and motivation. They've also added lovely sweetness and texture to many of my recipes, as you will discover in this chapter.

Like many baby boomers, I have an affinity for Bugs Bunny. He's one of my favorite cartoon characters. He is confident and calm, and an excellent problem-solver. He also has a sense of humor and looks out for the underdog. His famous line—"What's up, Doc?"—became so iconic that Warner Brothers trademarked it. Bugs Bunny took a leadership turn in the 1996 movie *Space Jam*, analyzing his competition (a nefarious basketball team) and developing a vision (including recruiting Michael Jordan, smart move) so that he and his cartoon allies could emerge victorious.

But perhaps above all, Bugs eats carrots. He eats so many carrots that I, along with most non-rabbit-owning people, believed that rabbits must, as a result, eat lots and lots of carrots. It was not until I became the unhappy owner of a rabbit named Smokey that I discovered the false narrative Bugs had built. (Did Warner Brothers own carrot farms?) On my first visit to the veterinarian with Smokey, I was informed that rabbits shouldn't eat carrots because they are too high in sugar. Bugs Bunny's ability to convince me and many others that rabbits ate carrots was a clear example of the power of association—and shows how people follow the lead of celebrities, even animated ones. No wonder these people have such an influence, even if we don't realize it.

Smokey arrived at our home unannounced before Easter in 1996, as a gift from one of my husband's sisters. Accepting this gift taught me that it is important to say no when your gut is saying no, even if the decision will be unpopular. We had a busy life, three children, two careers, and an ailing grandparent.

On day one, Smokey broke the fragile family equilibrium when my daughter dropped him so hard that he broke his foot. His injury softened my heart a bit, and for the next six months, I fed Smokey, cleaned his cage, and tried to show him some attention (as much attention you can give without touching).

That Thanksgiving, about six months into Smokey's tenure, we decided to head off for a much-needed vacation. One of my other sisters-in-law, who had a few rabbits of her own, agreed to watch

Smokey while we were away. The joy I felt when I dropped him off was profound. And I did not rush to my sister-in-law's house to retrieve him when we came home from the trip. In fact, I did not go at all. Christmas came and went. No one asked for Smokey, and I didn't remind anyone.

Smokey lived out the rest of his many days with his rabbit friends at my sister-in-law's. My only regret is that I didn't say no to Smokey right away. He could have had six additional months of bliss in a much better home environment.

In life and in business, say no when you mean no—and if you miss that opportunity, don't be afraid to change the plan. In the long run, it's best for everyone.

If you've ever tried to change your own or someone else's behavior, at work or at home, you have probably used the "carrot-and-stick" approach in some form. Reward the behavior or outcome you desire with something positive (a carrot) and discourage undesirable actions with negative reinforcement (a stick). A carrot can be additional compensation, time off, or any other gesture of appreciation. For example, the CEO of Caribou Coffee was once known for rewarding high-achieving employees with custom-designed Converse Chuck Taylor sneakers. The cloud-based contact management company Full-Contact has given select employees $7,500 to go on a paid vacation. A "stick," on the other hand, often comes in the form of a reduced bonus or a fine. For example, to ensure independence, employees in the financial services industry who fail to fully disclose their security holdings trading activity are subject to fines.

As a leader in higher education, I never found the "carrot-and-stick" approach all that helpful. At my institution, we had very few carrots (due to budgetary constraints and a focus on parity) and rarely employed the use of sticks (as a Jesuit, Catholic institution, we emphasized mercy and caring for the whole person). That said, we looked for potential carrots wherever we could find them.

One creative carrot came in the form of a biweekly email called "Good News Friday," in which we publicized good work from the faculty and staff and thanked them. It was a well-received carrot, but I noticed over time that we were often recognizing the same people. It drove home the importance of hiring people who are intrinsically motivated: those who derive their own private, invisible carrots simply from doing their work and doing it well.

Well-funded companies, on the other hand, have plenty of carrots around, leading to intriguing questions of how they can be used. In a 2008 paper in the *University of Miami Business Law Review*, Neil Newman proposed a carrot approach to financial statement preparation. As you know, top executives tend to get paid astronomical sums when their companies perform well financially. The salary-and-bonus carrot encourages them to foster growth, trim costs, and generally deliver for their shareholders. They receive no such carrot for presenting their financial statements accurately and well, however—only a stick, in the form of risking a Securities and Exchange Commission review.

Newman proposed that CEOs and CFOs receive incentive-based compensation based on financial statement accuracy rather than financial performance. It never caught on for a variety of valid reasons. But it's interesting to consider whether such an approach, or even a hybrid approach, could shift executives' emphasis from manipulating short-term performance to driving long-term performance, which could create greater stakeholder value.

My respect for carrots grew exponentially when I met Chester Elton, a motivational speaker and author of numerous books that have appeared on the *New York Times* bestseller lists. One of them, which I have read and applied in my own career, is *The Carrot Principle: How the Best Managers Use Recognition to Engage Their People, Retain Talent, and Accelerate Performance*. Elton is dynamic, insightful, and funny. He takes his love of the color orange—orange socks, orange ties, even orange roses for his wife—as well as his passion for carrots—as the subject of books and in plush toys—to a whole new level. Using carrots, Elton taught me the importance of building a culture of gratitude and helpfulness in my workplace. His idea is that the customer experience will never exceed the employee experience—so if you want your clients to perceive a reward in using your good or service, your employees had better feel satisfaction and reward in creating it.

Among the highest-utility aspects of Elton's work is his research into employee motivation. He argues that people each have different ideas of what a carrot is. In his book, *What Motivates Me? Put Your Passions to Work*, Elton puts forth a motivators assessment. I took the assessment and invited everyone who worked with me at the Gabelli School to take it as well. I found it fascinating and helpful.

Knowing what motivated my teammates helped me to be a better leader and manager. For some, it was having fun at work. (Not me—based on my responses, fun fell solidly at the bottom of the 32-item list). For others, it was opportunities for personal growth, knowing that your work has a tangible impact, or being able to support your family. Once I better understood what motivated my colleagues, we used that information to inspire activities for our staff-wide professional development days. One featured a yoga class, and another included a cooking workshop I led in which we all prepared tiramisu (page 164).

Leaders need to understand what motivates their employees most, and this diversity of carrots in the workplace reminded me that carrots actually come in many colors in addition to orange: purple, red, white, and yellow. Carrots for everyone!

The recipes that follow are delicious year round, but most are best served in the winter when you are looking to enjoy comfort food.

SPIKED CARROT JUICE (OR NOT)

Makes 1 drink

Prep Time: 10 minutes • Cook Time: 15 minutes

I recommend serving this super-refreshing drink either for brunch or lunch. I originally prepared it without any alcohol until one of my guests suggested that I "liven it up." Now I make it both ways. It is a wonderful mocktail for expectant mothers and the children in your life.

Tips to make it great:

Use fresh carrots.

Serve in a tall, chilled glass and add vodka.

INGREDIENTS

1 cup sliced carrots

1/2 cup pineapple juice

1/2 cup orange juice

1/2 teaspoon orange peel

2 cup ice cubes

1 ounce vodka (optional)

Pineapple wedge, for garnish

Orange peel, for garnish

INSTRUCTIONS

1   Place the sliced carrots in a medium pot of water, bring to a boil, and boil for 15 minutes, or until carrots are very soft. Strain the carrots and transfer to a bowl to cool for 5 minutes. (If you are pressed for time, you can use a can of cooked carrots.)

2   Once the carrots have cooled, place them in a blender or food processor along with the pineapple juice, orange juice, orange peel, and the ice. Blend until all ingredients are liquified.

3   If you want a little more excitement, add 1 ounce of vodka. Pour into a chilled glass and garnish with a pineapple wedge and orange peel.

AIR-FRIED CARROT CHIPS

Serves 4

Prep Time: 5 minutes

Cook Time: 10 minutes if using an air fryer, or 20 minutes if using a traditional oven

These are really easy to make and also fun to eat. If you're feeling adventurous, add some kale and make a potpourri of healthy chips. They are truly delicious and make a colorful pairing with the carrot juice on the previous page.

Tips to make it great:

Prepare a few dips, such as blue cheese salad dressing, hummus, or onion dip to pair with the chips.

To save time, buy a bag of pre-cut carrot slices. If there is a Wegmans supermarket near you, their brand is the perfect size and shape.

INGREDIENTS

1 teaspoon garlic powder

1 teaspoon adobo powder

1 teaspoon Himalayan pink salt

1 teaspoon black pepper

1-pound package raw carrot chips

3 tablespoons extra-virgin olive oil

INSTRUCTIONS

1   Preheat your air fryer or oven to 400 degrees F.

2   In a large plastic container with a lid, shake the spices and salt and pepper to blend, and then add carrots and oil to the container. Cover and shake it well for about 1 minute. The carrot chips should be glazed with the spice mixture.

3   If using an air fryer, place the carrots on the air fryer tray and bake for 5 minutes on each side. If using a traditional oven, coat a baking sheet with cooking oil spray or a light glaze of oil and bake the slices for 10 minutes on each side.

SPAGHETTI PRIMAVERA

Serves 3 to 4

Prep Time: 15 minutes

Cook Time: 20 minutes for sauce and 20 minutes for spaghetti

I started making this pasta for most holiday get-togethers I hosted many years ago when I learned that my cousin's daughter was vegetarian. She could possibly be "tricked" into eating Sunday gravy, but my conscience wouldn't allow it. Since then, it's been a mainstay second pasta to round out a menu.

Tips to make it great:

Cut the vegetables small but not too small.

Remember that the vegetables will keep cooking after you remove them from the stove, so it's best to cook them until a little firm.

Have plenty of extra vegetable broth on the side if you are not serving it immediately.

INGREDIENTS

3 carrots

1 large head of broccoli

1 zucchini, unpeeled

1 box cherry tomatoes

2 tablespoons butter

2 tablespoons extra-virgin olive oil

1 tablespoon Garlic Paste (page 17)

INSTRUCTIONS

1 Chop up all the vegetables into bite-size pieces. I usually start by peeling the carrots and cutting them into about 1/4-inch thick round slices. I then cut each round slice into quarters. Depending on how big the carrot is, though, I may only cut them in half.

2 Next, the broccoli. Cut off the florets from the stem and then quarter them. Peel the zucchini like the carrots, into 1/4-inch thick round slices and then quarter them. Finally, quarter the cherry tomatoes.

INGREDIENTS (cont.)

1 quart vegetable broth

Himalayan pink salt and pepper, to taste

1-pound spaghetti or angel hair (I use De Cecco spaghetti #12 or De Cecco angel hair #9)

1/4 cup iodized salt for boiling water

1/2 cup grated Parmigiano-Reggiano

INSTRUCTIONS (cont.)

3   As noted, the vegetables cook at their own pace, so be patient and cook them separately. Carrots and broccoli take longer, so I start with them. Add butter and olive oil to a large sauté pan over medium heat and add carrots. Cook until soft but crisp, remove from heat.

4   Add the broccoli and cook it the same. Once the broccoli is cooked, remove it and set it aside with the carrots. Cook the zucchini and then the cherry tomatoes the same way.

5   Once all of the vegetables are cooked, mix them together.

6   In a large pot over medium heat, add the garlic paste and vegetable broth. Once it is warm, add the vegetables, salt, and pepper and cook it all for 5 minutes.

7   Boil water for the spaghetti and once boiling, add iodized salt to the water. Cook the pasta until it is al dente. Depending on how much liquid is in the vegetables, you may want to hold back a cup of water from the boiling pasta.

8   When the pasta is done, strain it, add it to the pot of vegetables, and stir to thoroughly combine. Cover the pasta with the grated Parmigiano-Reggiano.

CARROT FAGIOLI SLIDERS

Serves 4

Prep Time: 20 minutes • Cook Time: 15–20 minutes

I began making these sliders for vegetarian guests in our home, and wouldn't you know they ended up being popular among the carnivores, too. High in vitamins and low in calories, they are delicious and nutritious treats!

Tips to make it great:

Patties can be prepared in advance and refrigerated.

Serve on a potato roll with a side of coleslaw.

INGREDIENTS

3 tablespoons extra-virgin olive oil, divided

3/4 cup panko-style breadcrumbs

1 small onion, diced

1 tablespoon tomato paste

1 1/2 teaspoons Himalayan pink salt, plus more to taste

4 large carrots, peeled and grated (about 2 cups)

1 (15-ounce) can of fagioli (cannellini or other white beans), drained and rinsed

Sprig of parsley, chopped

INSTRUCTIONS

1 Heat 1 tablespoon of olive oil in a large frying pan over low heat. Add the panko breadcrumbs and cook, stirring regularly, for about 4 minutes. The breadcrumbs will become crispy. Remove them from the heat and transfer them to a large bowl.

2 Using the same frying pan, add the remaining 2 tablespoons of olive oil, the diced garlic, and the onion. Cook the onion for about 8 minutes, stirring occasionally, until soft and golden brown. Add the tomato paste, salt, and carrots, and cook for an additional 8 minutes, stirring frequently, until the carrots are very soft.

3 Transfer this mixture to the bowl with the cooked panko. Add the drained beans. Using a wooden spoon, stir until all contents are mixed. The texture should be gooey, but I prefer the beans to be mostly intact.

INGREDIENTS (cont.)

Freshly ground black pepper, to taste

1 extra large egg, beaten

1 tablespoon diced garlic

Package of potato rolls

INSTRUCTIONS (cont.)

4   Add parsley, pepper, and more salt. Next, mix in the raw egg. Shape into 8 evenly sized balls and then flatten them into slider-sized patties when you are ready to cook.

5   For cooking, coat a flat pan with cooking oil spray or olive oil and put over medium heat. Transfer the sliders to the pan, cover it with a lid, and cook for 3 minutes on each side. Serve sliders on potato rolls. If you like, you can offer mayonnaise as a dressing option.

MISO BUTTER CARROTS

Serves 4

Prep Time: 5 minutes • Cook Time: 20 minutes

This bright orange dish looks as good as it tastes. Children have been known to think they're eating candy as they dig into these carrots.

Tips to make it great:

Consider adding sesame seeds after the carrots are cooked.

Use Kerrygold butter.

INGREDIENTS

2 tablespoons unsalted butter, softened

1 1/2 teaspoons miso paste

1 1/2 tablespoons extra-virgin olive oil

Pinch of Himalayan pink salt

8 carrots, washed and peeled (I like to use a variety of colors)

1/2 teaspoon honey

INSTRUCTIONS

1   Preheat the oven to 400 degrees F.

2   Mix the softened butter and miso paste together in a small bowl.

3   Rub the olive oil and salt into the carrots, place them on a baking sheet, and bake for 10 minutes.

4   Remove from the oven, pour half of the miso butter and all of the honey onto the carrots, and bake for an additional 8 to 10 minutes. Right before serving, pour the remaining miso butter over the carrots.

CARROT CAKE

Prep Time: 20 minutes to prepare batter, 10 additional minutes to frost cake

Cook Time: 45 minutes

Yes, this cake takes a bit of effort, but word to the wise, I never feel guilty eating this dessert. The carrots and raisins are packed with vitamins, and the cake is a real crowd-pleaser.

Tips to make it great:

Make sure the eggs are at room temperature.

Peel and grate the carrots yourself rather than buying a bag of shredded carrots.

Pan Prep

———

Butter, for greasing

All-purpose flour, for dusting

(continued on next page)

INGREDIENTS

Batter

2 cups all-purpose flour

2 teaspoons baking soda

1/2 teaspoon Himalayan pink salt

1 1/2 teaspoons ground cinnamon

1 1/4 cups vegetable oil

1 cup granulated sugar

1 cup lightly packed brown sugar

1 teaspoon vanilla extract

4 extra large eggs at room temperature

6 medium carrots, peeled and grated
(about 3 cups)

1/2 cup raisins

1/2 cup chopped walnuts or pecans
(optional)

Frosting

8 ounces cream cheese at room temperature

1 1/4 cups powdered sugar

1/3 cup heavy cream

INSTRUCTIONS

1 Position a rack in the middle of the oven and preheat the oven to 350 degrees F.

2 Grease two 9-inch round cake pans with butter, then flour the bottom and sides of both pans. Tap out any remaining flour. Be sure to fully cover the bottom and sides with both butter and flour.

3 For the batter, whisk the flour, baking soda, salt, and cinnamon in a medium bowl (bowl 1) until fully incorporated. In a separate bowl (bowl 2), whisk the oil, granulated sugar, brown sugar, and vanilla extract. Add the eggs to bowl 2, one at a time, whisking after each one. Use a large rubber spatula to scrape the sides and bottom of bowl 2.

4 Gradually add the contents of bowl 1 into bowl 2, gently stirring until they disappear and the batter is smooth. Stir in the carrots and raisins, and if you like nuts in your carrot cake, now is a good time to stir in chopped walnuts or pecans.

5 Divide the cake batter between the two prepared cake pans.

6 Bake until the tops of the cake layers are springy when touched and when a toothpick inserted into the center of them comes out clean, about 35 to 45 minutes.

7 Cool the cakes in the pans for 30 minutes, then carefully turn the cake layers out onto cooling racks.

8 While the cakes cool, make the frosting. In a large bowl, beat the cream cheese with a handheld mixer on medium speed until smooth, for about 1 minute. Beat in the powdered sugar, 1/4 cup at a time, and after all the sugar has been incorporated, pour in the whipping cream. Beat on medium speed for 2 to 3 minutes, or until the frosting is whipped and creamy. This frosting should have a texture that's close to whipped cream. Cover and chill until you are ready to frost the cake.

Frosting and Serving

———

1   When the cake layers are completely cool (usually 1 hour or more), frost the top of one cake layer and place the second cake layer on top.

2   Frost the top of the second layer. I usually don't frost the sides of this cake, but you should have enough frosting if you would like to do so.

3   Place on a large platter and serve at room temperature. Enjoy!

7

Shake the Salt

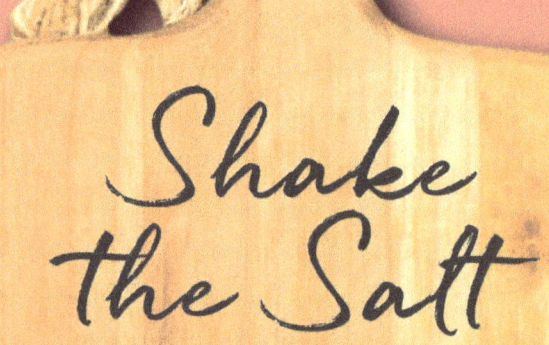

Salty Dog

Salty Guacamole

Salt (and Pepper) Shrimp

Syracuse Salt Potatoes

Salt-Encrusted Filet Mignon Roast

Lisa's Peanut Butter Pie with Nutty Salt Topping

While I greatly appreciate the added value that many spices bring to recipes, I'm absolutely in awe of salt. I don't remember exactly when or why I fell in love with it. Perhaps it was the numerous individual salt shakers that were on our holiday tables or my infatuation with the Morton Salt girl. I remember running around in front of our house holding an umbrella, pretending to be her.

Over time, I grew to appreciate the incredibly diverse set of functions salt can play: it can melt ice, it can (according to my mom and others) ward off evil spirits, and it can serve as a valuable business metaphor, providing insights into professional topics from brand recognition to building high-performing teams. But what has always stood out to me is salt's ability to enhance the existing flavor of food. It's remarkably good at that.

My family used two types of iodized salt growing up: Red Cross and Morton. Both are iconic brands that have been popular for more than 100 years, and one or both were always in the house. We used them generously in cooking, and my mother kept extra on hand in case someone moved into a new home or apartment. To this day, she delivers a carton of salt, holy water, and a broom to anyone's new residence to ward off and sweep away any evil spirits.

I personally made sure our salt inventory went to good use. Did I deploy it before tasting the food first? You bet. That's because 98 percent of the time, it's the right move. Immediate salting calls forth the full flavor of the food. Why waste a morsel?

I'm aware that some people believe that salting your food before sampling signals impulsiveness, untrustworthiness, or disrespect. For anyone who knows me, those labels just don't fit. And that is just a friendly reminder that stereotypes aren't helpful. I make salt piles to dip my steak in. I find it ridiculous when chefs don't allow salt on the table. I understand that a chef strives to prepare a perfectly seasoned dish, but everyone has a different palate and tolerance to salt. I believe in giving people the choice.

The first connection I discovered between salt and business is that the word "salt" and the word "salary" share the same root. You likely have read references to individuals long ago being paid in salt; it was an immensely valuable asset around the world—more valuable than gold to some, because having salt to preserve food meant that you could eat year round. You could survive.

It was considered so valuable, in fact, that spilling salt became a bad omen, like breaking a mirror. It probably explains why, in our family, if you dropped a significant amount of salt on the table or floor, you needed to shake more salt over your shoulder.

Reading books and articles by Ed Krow helped me to draw even deeper connections between salt and business—in particular, leadership. Krow uses the acronym "SALT" to outline what I consider to be some of the most important leadership actions: serve, appreciate, listen, trust.

His approach to the second of those, appreciation, stresses how important it is to show that sentiment in a meaningful, personal way. A gift of appreciation for a colleague who has small children might be something for the family (a box of cupcakes, a board game, or a hot chocolate maker—some gifts that I've given personally); for someone who enjoys going out and trying new things, it might be a restaurant gift card.

The more your gesture of appreciation aligns personally with the receiver, the more likely it will demonstrate your gratitude in an authentic way. In my academic career, I sought to positively influence the culture at Fordham University by sharing heartfelt notes and gifts with people whose contributions or presence I deeply appreciated. In turn, I was beyond grateful when I received thoughtful gifts of appreciation at the end of my tenure as dean, including books (I'm a book lover) and a dinner at Babbo (a restaurant owned by one of my favorite chefs and authors, Lidia Bastianich).

Let's revisit Ed Krow's take on SALT for a moment. Krow drove home the need for a measured hand when leading a team. Humans need salt to live, but applied too heavily, it can indeed ruin food. Likewise, when leaders insert themselves *too much* at work, productivity and creativity can be negatively impacted.

In the kitchen, I've oversalted spinach on more than one occasion. The most embarrassing time was on a holiday, when I should have thrown the dish out but decided to serve it anyway, leading to 13 out of 14 plates of uneaten greens (the exception being my brother-in-law, who eats everything, and who commented "the spinach is a little salty . . ." as he ate more than his share).

In the workplace, the element of SALT that is most needed can be the "T"—good teams are best served when leaders trust their people to do the job well. Reduced intervention can produce exceptional outcomes. Very often, I saw my Gabelli School colleagues thrive in this way. I invited my team to develop a staff wellness day, and they planned a restorative event that featured a "calming room" with relaxing lighting, scents, and music. It evolved into an annual event, and its creators became strong advocates for keeping that room as a permanent fixture.

By pulling back, leaders can also bring out the talent of those they work with. I recall the compelling admissions presentations that team members created when given the latitude and creative freedom to put together something unique. Greater autonomy allows each person to be authentic and to bring their distinct talents and perspective to problem-solving and innovating.

When cooking, I always thought that if you added too much salt, it was hopeless. But there are remedies! Try adding an acid, such as lemon juice or apple cider vinegar. Stir in some sour cream when you overdo the salt in mashed potatoes (done that). If you oversalt a stew, simply add more potatoes.

When it comes to work, the same principle applies: if you insert yourself too much or micromanage, step back and give your team autonomy. (Also, apologize if necessary.) You might find that the team comes up with better ideas with a little breathing room.

When it comes to adding salt, either in business or in cooking, "timing is everything." Bill Gross, the founder and CEO of Idea Lab, the longest-running technology incubator, artfully explains in his 2015 TED Talk that the most important factor in a startup's success is timing, and that goes for bigger businesses and their initiatives, too. A great idea and good execution are important, but they have to come at the right time.

In the kitchen, *when* you add salt can have a significant impact on the outcome of your recipe. In general, adding salt slowly throughout the cooking process is best, seasoning as you add each ingredient. Waiting until your pasta water boils to add salt and adding salt to each bite of a tomato gives the best flavor!

Salt has more recently turned me into a "brand advocate." As you probably know, several types of salt are used in cooking, among them iodized table salt, sea salt, and Kosher salt. But my absolute favorite salt—the only salt I use now, as you may have guessed from the recipes in this book—is one that I discovered while enjoying a cooking class in Greece: Himalayan pink salt.

Extracted from the Khewra Salt Mines near the Himalayas in Pakistan, this pink salt is believed to have been formed millions of years ago from the evaporation of ancient bodies of water. It has more minerals than iodized salt and, in my opinion, enhances the flavor of food more. I have made many friends and family members advocates for pink salt, and my work continues.

Finally, the phrase "back to the salt mines" has taken on new meaning for me since I stepped down from my position as dean of the Gabelli School and returned to being a faculty member. As dean, I had always found myself referring to the salt mines when it was time to return to mind-numbing meetings (often during budgeting season). Lately, I have been thinking that if it were a salt mine in the Himalayas, it might not be so bad.

Note: Too much salt can cause you to become thirsty. Saratoga sparkling water is my family favorite. Keep the blue bottle on hand when you enjoy these recipes. I don't want any emergency-room trips due to salt-induced dehydration!

SALTY DOG

Makes 1 cocktail

Prep Time: 5 minutes

This cocktail is one of my husband's go-to drinks (although he doesn't call it a Salty Dog). He enjoys it in a rocks glass with two or three large ice cubes.

Tips to make it great:

Use a splash of pink grapefruit juice.

Serve over ice.

INGREDIENTS

1 lime wedge, for the rim

Himalayan pink salt, for salting the rim

3 ounces vodka

1/4 cup pink grapefruit juice

6 ice cubes

1 lemon wedge, for garnish

Grapefruit peel curl for garnish (optional)

INSTRUCTIONS

1   Prepare the glass (a rocks glass or martini glass) by generously rubbing the rim with lime. Pour Himalayan pink salt into a small flat dish. I prefer rolling the outside of the rim in the dish, but if you want the added salt flavor in your drink, you can dip the rim into the salt like you would a cookie cutter. Fill the glass with a few large ice cubes.

2   Pour the vodka and the grapefruit juice into a shaker filled with ice.

3   Shake for one minute. Pour the contents of the shaker into the salted and ice-filled glass. Garnish with a lemon wedge.

SALTY GUACAMOLE

Serves 6

Prep Time: 10 minutes

Our family was late to the avocado party. It wasn't until our children were young adults that we started serving and enjoying it. These days, my granddaughters have been known to just about smother themselves in it. This Salty Guacamole is my daughter Danielle's recipe. And even though we all follow her recipe, hers always comes out the best.

Tips to make it great:

Use fresh lime juice.

Save the pit from one avocado, and once you are finished making the guacamole, place the pit in the center of the bowl with the guacamole to keep it from turning brown.

Use ripe, room-temperature avocados.

INGREDIENTS

4 ripe avocados, peeled, pitted, and chopped

1 large ripe tomato, chopped

1 tablespoon minced garlic

Half a jalapeño pepper, finely chopped

1/2 small red onion, finely chopped

2 tablespoons Himalayan pink salt

1 teaspoon black pepper

1/2 cup fresh cilantro, finely chopped

2 tablespoons freshly squeezed lime juice

INSTRUCTIONS

1   If you have a molcajete bowl and a pestle, now is the time to use it. Otherwise, a large bowl and wooden spoon will work.

2   Place the avocado in the bowl and mash them. Next, add the tomato and do the same.

3   Mix in the garlic, jalapeno, and onion. Finally, add salt, pepper, cilantro, and lime juice. Mix well, but don't overdo it. You want some texture to the dip. Place a saved pit in the center of the bowl and serve with Tostitos corn chips.

SALT (AND PEPPER) SHRIMP

Serves 4 to 5

Prep Time: 15 to 25 minutes, depending on whether or not shrimp are already cleaned

Cook time: 7 minutes

The first time I enjoyed this dish was at the New York City restaurant Chin Chin on 49th Street (long since closed), which, as I mentioned in Chapter 3, also served a wonderful Peking Duck. The owner Jimmy Chin was always happy to share his recipes, so now you can join me in being grateful for his good taste *and* his generosity.

Tips to make it great:

Use fresh lemon.

Choose extra-large shrimp.

Prepare cherry peppers as a side dish.

INGREDIENTS

20 extra-large shrimp (try for U 10, which means under 10 shrimp per pound)

2 extra large eggs

1/4 cup whole milk

1/4 cup club soda

1 cup all-purpose flour

1/4 cup corn starch

1/4 cup seasoned breadcrumbs

INSTRUCTIONS

1   If you need to clean the shrimp, I find it easiest to use food scissors to cut through the back of the shrimp's shell, making it easier to peel the shell off. Try to keep the very edge of the shell on the tail. It will look nicer when you serve. Wash the shrimp well to remove any black residue. Place the clean shrimp on a paper towel–lined plate.

2   In a medium bowl, add the egg, milk, and club soda and mix thoroughly. In another large bowl, add the flour, cornstarch, breadcrumbs, salt, and pepper.

INGREDIENTS (cont.)

2 teaspoons Himalayan pink salt

1 teaspoon black pepper

Extra-virgin olive oil (amount varies depending on if you fry or air fry; no oil is needed if you air fry or bake the shrimp)

INSTRUCTIONS (cont.)

3   One by one, dip the shrimp into the egg mix bowl, and then into the flour mix, and transfer to a tray or cutting board. Once all of the shrimp have been coated, they are ready to be cooked.

4   You have three choices for cooking: fry, bake, or air fry.

To fry: Fill your large sauté pan one-quarter of the way with extra-virgin olive oil. Once the oil is heated (drop a bit of the flour mixture in, and if it bubbles up, it's hot enough), put the shrimp in. Don't overcrowd them. Turn them after 2 to 3 minutes; it only takes about 5 minutes in total to cook the shrimp.

To bake: Preheat the oven to 400 degrees F. Spray a baking sheet with cooking oil spray. Place the shrimp in the pan, and again, don't overcrowd them. They should take 7 or 8 minutes to cook. I always check them after 5 minutes and turn them over.

To Air Fry: Place the shrimp in the air fry tray and lightly spray a bit of olive oil over them using an oil spritzer (oil misto). Leave in for 5 minutes and then check them. They will have turned orange when they are done. It usually takes 7 or 8 minutes for them to fully cook.

SYRACUSE SALT POTATOES

Serves 4 to 6

Prep Time: 5 minutes

Cook Time: 20 minutes

My son-in-law, who is from the Syracuse area (also known as Salt City), introduced me to this classic, regional recipe. It's incredible how simple yet delicious it is. In upstate New York, stores often sell the potatoes and the salt for this dish together in one bag. I use either small red potatoes or small multicolored potatoes for this recipe.

Tips to make it great:

Use a large pot that holds plenty of water.

Use Kerrygold Irish salted butter.

INGREDIENTS

3 pounds new potatoes (small potatoes; I often use red ones)

1 1/4 cup iodized salt

1/2 cup melted Kerrygold salted butter

INSTRUCTIONS

1   Wash the potatoes well. Fill a large pot with water and add the salt. Put the potatoes in the pot and then bring to a boil. Once boiling, cook the potatoes for 15 minutes, until they are easily pierced with a fork. Drain and cover.

2   Melt the butter in a nonstick pan. Pour over the potatoes and serve immediately.

SALT-ENCRUSTED FILET MIGNON ROAST

Serves 6 to 8

Prep Time: 10 minutes

Cook Time: 20 to 30 minutes

In our family, this filet mignon, "cooked like a roast beef," is at every single holiday meal. I often have two on hand! It cooks quickly enough so I can read the crowd to decide whether and when to put a second one in to roast.

Tips to make it great:

> Coat the meat with olive oil.
>
> Serve with *au jus* brown gravy.
>
> Remember, the meat keeps cooking after you take it out of the oven, and you can't "uncook" overcooked meat. So err on the rare side.

INGREDIENTS

7-pound filet mignon roast

3 tablespoons extra-virgin olive oil

1/4 cup Himalayan pink salt

1/4 cup black pepper

INSTRUCTIONS

1. Preheat the oven to 500 degrees F.

2. Rub the filet mignon roast with the oil. Pour the salt into a sizeable pan or onto an extra-large cutting board and roll the filet mignon over the salt until it is entirely encrusted. Next, pour the pepper onto the cutting board and roll the filet in the pepper and what remains of the salt. Set the filet mignon aside to rest at room temperature for 1 hour.

(continued on next page)

INSTRUCTIONS (cont.)

3　When you are ready to roast it, place the filet mignon in the pan with the fat side on top. Transfer it to the oven and immediately lower the oven temperature to 350 degrees F. Roast for 20 to 30 minutes at 350 degrees.

4　Check the thermometer for temperature. For rare, you'll want it to read 120 degrees F, and for medium, 130 degrees F. Remember: the meat continues to cook a bit after it is out of the oven, so I always err on the rarer side.

5　Let rest for 10 minutes before cutting the roast into roughly 1 1/2 inch slices. I generally pour a small amount of *au jus* gravy on top, but it isn't essential.

LISA'S PEANUT BUTTER PIE WITH NUTTY SALT TOPPING

Serves 6 or 1, depending on the audience

Prep Time: 15 minutes

My sister-in-law Lisa makes this no-bake pie that always garners rave reviews. In fact, my son has been known to take the pie and put it in the basement so no one else can have any. Seriously. Recently, she made him an entire pie for his birthday, which he ate in one sitting!

Tips to make it great:

Ask Lisa to make it for you!

Be sure your heavy cream is very cold before whipping.

Be sure the cream cheese is soft.

INGREDIENTS

8 ounces softened cream cheese

1/2 cup granulated sugar

1/4 cup creamy peanut butter

1 tablespoon whole milk

1 cup heavy cream, whisked until fluffy

1 9-inch chocolate pie crust (Keebler and Oreo are both good options)

1/4 cup chopped peanuts

1 chocolate bar, shaved

1 tablespoon Himalayan pink salt

INSTRUCTIONS

1 In a large bowl, combine the softened cream cheese, sugar, peanut butter, and milk, and stir until blended.

2 Fold in the whipped cream and mix well.

3 Transfer the pie filling into the crust, and refrigerate and chill for at least 2 hours.

4 Top evenly with the chopped peanuts, shaved chocolate, and salt right before serving.

Try It, It's Chicken

8

Chicken Soup Hot Toddy

Chicken Soup

Chicken Cacciatore (Chicken, Hunter's Style)

Arugula Salad with Chicken

Chicken Fried Rice

Brussels Sprouts with Chicken and Bacon (Triple Decker Sprouts)

Tavuk Gögsü (Turkish Chicken Bread Pudding)

As a child, I was often labeled a "chicken" which, in my humble opinion, was generally unwarranted as I was pretty brave (I once fought off a group of kids who were trying to take my older brother's bike). That said, I earned the name thanks to my general aversion to insects and a few late-night encounters with so-called monsters in my closet. I was also a regular loser at the game known as "chicken." I'd always do a quick risk-versus-reward analysis and choose to step aside. To this day, I favor compromise.

These early negative associations with chicken were reinforced by my father, who generally refused to eat it, calling it a "dirty bird." As a result, the only chicken dishes I remember eating growing up were chicken soup and chicken cacciatore with spaghetti. No chicken cutlets, no barbeque chicken, no Chicken Française, no oven-roasted chicken. Those dishes didn't become favorites until much, much later in my life.

My husband didn't help my impression of chicken, either. He had interacted with the "dirty bird" firsthand as a child thanks to a chicken coop his grandmother kept in her yard in Italy. He was usually the one responsible for cracking the chickens' necks and also for de-feathering them. Chicken, therefore, was not something he would eat.

Given how stacked the deck was against chicken, it's amazing that these days I thoroughly enjoy eating and cooking it. I've also taken numerous leadership lessons from this intelligent bird!

Chickens are indeed intelligent, emotional animals with individual personalities. Scientists have conducted numerous studies that find chickens to be masters of manipulation and counterstrategies, with males making false food calls to attract nearby females, and females eventually ignoring those who make false alerts too often. Chickens are also empathic; they understand the importance of knowing their flock, and they use past experiences to make decisions. They also pass down knowledge from generation to generation, if given the chance.

Expressing empathy, knowing your team members, learning from the past, and sharing your knowledge are all essential leadership skills. Perhaps we need more chickens in leadership roles?

I didn't truly appreciate chicken until after my children were born and our pediatrician encouraged me to make their baby food. One important protein she suggested I prepare was chicken. For them, I'd sauté the chicken in a pan or boil it and then pass it through a food mill (the same one my grandmother used to get the seeds out of tomatoes). If I was making a large batch, I'd freeze the cooked chicken in ice cube trays and then pop out a cube a day. In that process, I discovered that the chicken—surprise, surprise—tasted good.

As our children grew older, their friends all enjoyed chicken cutlets over veal cutlets, and they loved Boston Market chicken (I appreciated the variety of side dishes). Their favorite dish was Chicken Française. I learned to make chicken salad from soup chicken, Southern fried chicken, and chicken teriyaki (one too many times). I even convinced my husband to make barbeque chicken.

Meanwhile, as chicken became a regular at the dinner table, the phrase "pecking order" began to come up at work; when I started my career at Fordham University, I was reminded that I was at the bottom. The more senior professors were given the preferred courses and had outsized influence over the curriculum. At the time, I didn't realize that the phrase "pecking order" comes from the behavior of chickens—that they will peck at those lower than them to convey dominance.

As you already know, I was never a fan of the game "chicken," and my disdain for it grew along with my leadership responsibilities. I did not enjoy facing off with colleagues in an antagonistic way, holding out to see who would yield at the last minute. I saw how polarizing it could be, and the resulting outcomes were never optimal. Building a culture where collaboration is central to the organization is definitely the best way to go.

The most helpful work-related information that chickens provided me came through Margaret Heffernan, a CEO, entrepreneur, and author. Heffernan has delivered many famous TED Talks: "Dare to Disagree," "The Human Skills We Need in an Unpredictable World," and one of my personal favorites, "Forget the Pecking Order at Work." I was teaching a class of honors business students when I came across the latter, and it has been continually relevant since. Every time I watch the recording, I discover a new connection.

Heffernan says that organizations are known for boosting a few superstars to the top of the workplace pecking order and giving them all the resources and power. She argues that this is not the best approach. To back up that assertion, she draws a comparison with the animal world: specifically, a productivity experiment that biologist William Muir did with chickens.

Muir separated a flock of chickens into two groups based on the number of eggs they produced: one for average layers, and the other for high-volume producers, or "super chickens." He observed the birds for six generations, and the differences were notable. The second generation of the average group was plump, healthy, and laying more eggs than their forebears. In the "super chicken" group, only three were left alive—all the others had been pecked to death.

Heffernan connects this experiment to the workplace, citing MIT research that shows that high-performing teams are not likely to resemble the "super chickens"; instead, they allow everyone to contribute equally, with no one member dominating (or seeking dominance) and everyone having a voice. The best-performing teams also had more women members (love that).

At Fordham, as well as at other academic institutions, I saw several great curriculum innovations succeed and several get derailed. The most successful curricular change during my tenure as dean started with an overnight planning event offsite and continued with annual kick-off sessions to create community among the faculty. The ideas that got derailed were often because the leader of the initiative didn't allow other voices to be heard or tried to complete the project unilaterally. As Heffernan points out, competition and careless ambition can lead to negativity in the work environment. Collaboration is the best way to build social capital, get to know the people you work with, and bring out their strengths for the good of everyone.

I can think of another great way to get to know others: gathering for a great meal. Perhaps the recipes in this section—all hearty meals enjoyed most by my family on cold days—will inspire a meal with your coworkers. No "super chickens" necessary.

CHICKEN SOUP HOT TODDY

Makes 1 cocktail

Prep Time: 5 minutes

This winter drink will have you wondering why anyone needs a fireplace. It might sound strange to mix chicken broth with gin, but I promise you will get hooked from the very first sip.

Tips to make it great:

Serve in a brandy snifter.

Use fresh lemon juice.

INGREDIENTS

1 ounce gin (I use Beefeater, but the original recipe calls for Nolet's)

1 teaspoon fresh lemon juice

4 ounces hot chicken stock

1 dash celery bitters (available on Amazon or in most supermarkets)

Carrot stick, for garnish

Celery stick, for garnish

INSTRUCTIONS

1   Pour the gin, chicken stock, celery bitters, and lemon juice into the snifter and stir with a spoon.

2   Add the celery stick and carrot stick for garnish and serve.

CHICKEN SOUP

Serves 10

Prep Time: 30 minutes • Cook Time: 2 hours

I have been known to triple this recipe using two huge pots on many a winter Sunday. When I make such a large batch, I always share quarts with friends and family. My children have also bartered with this soup as currency over the years. The texture and flavor of the ground vegetables really make this soup memorable. It took me a few years to realize that you need to grind the vegetables up before cooking them for the best flavor.

Tips to make it great:

> Add a splash of red wine to the soup before serving.
>
> Freeze whatever you don't use.

INGREDIENTS

3 carrots

1 onion

2 cloves garlic

1 tomato

1 potato

1 package soup greens (this generally includes carrots, celery, parsnips, parsley, and a potato; I remove any thyme if it's part of the package, as it overpowers the soup)

10 cups chicken broth

INSTRUCTIONS

1 Use a large pot (10 to 12 quarts) or Dutch oven.

2 Peel all of the vegetables and rinse them before chopping into medium-sized pieces. Place all of the chopped vegetables and the package of soup greens, along with some of the vegetable broth, in a blender and blend until the vegetables are fine.

3 Once blended, pour into the large pot or Dutch oven. Continue this process in batches until all the vegetables are blended.

(continued on next page)

INGREDIENTS (cont.)

1 whole chicken, about 3 to 4 pounds (I remove and discard the internal organs, but you can leave them in if you prefer)

1 cup beef consommé (optional)

Himalayan pink salt, to taste

Black pepper, to taste

1/2 pound of pasta (I like to use De Cecco #78)

Parmigiano-Reggiano, for serving

INSTRUCTIONS (cont.)

4   Add the whole chicken, any remaining broth that you didn't use to blend the vegetables, and the beef consommé (optional). Fill the pot close to the top with water. Bring to a boil over high heat, and boil for 10 minutes. Reduce heat and simmer for about 2 hours. When done, the chicken meat should fall off the bone. Transfer the chicken to a large bowl to cool.

5   Boil the pasta and add it to the soup. Shred the chicken into the soup right before you serve it, and top with grated Parmigiano-Reggiano.

CHICKEN CACCIATORE (CHICKEN, HUNTER'S STYLE)

Serves 4 to 6

Prep Time: 20 minutes

Cook Time: 100 minutes (10 minutes for braising, 90 minutes for cooking)

I've enjoyed eating this tomato and garlicky dish since I was a child. "Cacciatore" means "hunter" in Italian, and legend has it that the dish was typically prepared after Italian aristocracy returned from hunting. It's hearty, delicious, and lucky for you, quite easy to make.

Tips to make it great:

Cook for a long time over a low flame.

Use drinking wine rather than cooking wine.

You can add potatoes and skip the pasta.

INGREDIENTS

4 pounds chicken cut into 8 pieces (I ask the butcher to cut the chicken up for me)

1/4 cup extra-virgin olive oil, divided

1 tablespoon chopped garlic, divided

1 red bell pepper, thinly sliced

1/3 cup onion, thinly sliced

1/4 cup red wine (I use Chianti — Pepoli is my go-to — or Cabernet Sauvignon, depending on what, if anything, is open at the time)

INSTRUCTIONS

1   Wash the chicken and pat it dry completely. In a large nonstick frying pan, add 2 tablespoons of the extra virgin olive oil and heat over medium-high. Add 1/2 tablespoon of the garlic. Brown the chicken pieces on both sides and transfer to a paper towel-lined plate.

2   Using the same pan, add the red peppers first and then, as they soften, the onion. Once the peppers and onions are lightly browned, transfer to a bowl and set aside.

(continued on next page)

INGREDIENTS (cont.)

2 boxes strained tomatoes

1 pound of pasta (I like De Cecco #12 spaghetti or De Cecco #15 bucatini)

Sprig of parsley, chopped

1 teaspoon Himalayan pink salt

1/2 teaspoon black pepper

INSTRUCTIONS (cont.)

3   In an 8-quart pot over medium-high heat, add the remaining olive oil and chopped garlic. Once the pot is hot, add the chicken, peppers, onions, wine, and tomatoes, and stir to combine with a wooden spoon. Add the parsley, salt, and pepper. Bring the sauce to a boil for 5 minutes, then lower to a simmer, and stir frequently for 90 minutes. The chicken will be very tender once done and should be almost falling off the bone.

4   When the chicken has about 20 minutes left, bring a large pot of water to a boil. Once boiling, add iodized salt. Once the water is boiling again, add one pound of De Cecco #12 spaghetti or De Cecco #15 bucatini. (The recipe will work with other pasta brands as well.) Cook the pasta until al dente.

5   Right before you strain the pasta, use a ladle to take two scoops of sauce (try not to get too many peppers or onions) and pour them into a large bowl. Strain the pasta, add it to the large bowl, and mix thoroughly. Place the chicken on a flat platter covered with the peppers, onion, and sauce. I like to put the pasta in one bowl and the chicken on a platter. This allows you to mix the pasta easily without having the chicken fall off the bone.

ARUGULA SALAD WITH CHICKEN

Serves 4

Prep Time: 20 minutes

Cook Time: 10 minutes

Arugula is full of antioxidants, and it's credited with reducing inflammation and being an excellent source of vitamin K. So, it's a win-win when you make this tasty salad. It can become a meal if you pair it with a loaf of crusty seeded bread.

Tips to make it great:

> Add shaved Parmigiano-Reggiano.
>
> Squeeze lemon on top of the salad after you dress it.

INGREDIENTS

Salad

1 pound boneless chicken breast

4 cups arugula

1 small red bell pepper

1 tablespoon Himalayan pink salt

1 teaspoon black peppercorns

1 lemon: half to season the serving bowl and half to squeeze into the dressing

3 pieces Parmigiano-Reggiano, for shaving

INSTRUCTIONS

1   Fill a 4-quart pot with water and bring to a boil. Once the water is boiling, add iodized salt and let it boil again. Add the peppercorns to the boiling water. Squeeze half of the lemon into the water and then toss in the squeezed fruit itself. Next, add the chicken. Once the water returns to a boil, lower the heat to a simmer, cover, and cook for 10 minutes. You don't want to overcook the chicken, but you don't want it to be pink, either.

2   Once the chicken is cooked, transfer it to a cutting board and set aside.

(continued on next page)

INGREDIENTS (cont.)

Dressing

1 tablespoon red wine vinegar

1 tablespoon balsamic vinegar

1/4 cup extra-virgin olive oil

1 teaspoon Dijon mustard

INSTRUCTIONS (cont.)

3   Before making the salad, prepare the serving bowl by rubbing the bowl with the remaining half of the lemon. Put the piece of lemon aside so that you can use it again to squeeze over the salad at the end.

4   Rinse the arugula leaves and use a salad spinner or paper towels to make sure it is totally dry. Place the greens in the serving bowl. Dice the red pepper into small squares and layer over the arugula.

5   Make the dressing in a separate small bowl. First, add the red wine and balsamic vinegar. Next, add the olive oil and Dijon mustard, then squeeze in the juice of the remaining half lemon. Use a whisk to fully blend and emulsify the dressing.

6   By now, the chicken should be cool and ready to be diced into small chunks. Chop up the chicken and layer it onto the salad. Add the dressing and mix well. As noted in the tips section above, enhance the salad by shaving Parmigiano-Reggiano on top.

CHICKEN FRIED RICE

Serves 6 to 8

Prep Time: 15 minutes • Cook Time: 30 minutes

This savory side dish can complete any meal or be the center of a meal if you toss up a salad to go with it.

Tips to make it great:

> Have patience when making this dish. By adding the ingredients one at a time, the rice will have more flavor.
>
> Let the rice sit for a while after you've completed the cooking process to let the flavors develop. If the rice gets cold, add a little water to the frying pan and reheat before serving.

INGREDIENTS

4 cups cooked white or brown rice

3 tablespoons extra-virgin olive oil, divided

3 chicken breasts, about 1 1/2 pounds

3 tablespoons low-sodium soy sauce

3 extra large eggs, beaten

2 carrots, peeled and diced

1 tablespoon freshly minced ginger

1 medium onion, chopped

INSTRUCTIONS

1 Cook the rice according to the package directions and set aside to cool.

2 In a large sauté or frying pan, add 1 tablespoon of the olive oil and sauté the chicken breast for 6 to 7 minutes until fully cooked. Remove and place on a cutting board to cool.

3 Add 1 more tablespoon of the olive oil to the pan and sauté the diced vegetables, adding the carrots first, then the ginger and onions, and finally the peas. Once the vegetables are fully cooked, remove them from the heat and place them in a very large bowl.

(continued on next page)

INGREDIENTS (cont.)

3/4 cup frozen peas

Himalayan pink salt to taste

Freshly ground black pepper to taste

INSTRUCTIONS (cont.)

4   Dice the cooked chicken and add it to the bowl with the vegetables, then add the rice. Begin mixing everything together, adding salt, pepper, and soy sauce to taste as you go.

5   Add the final tablespoon of olive oil to the pan and place it over low to medium heat. Once the pan is hot, crack the eggs into it and scramble them until fully cooked. Add the rice and chicken bowl mix to the pan and cook for 2 to 3 minutes. If you have time, use the advice in the tips section to enhance your rice's overall flavor.

BRUSSELS SPROUTS WITH CHICKEN AND BACON (TRIPLE DECKER SPROUTS)

Serves 4

Prep Time: 10 minutes • Cook Time: 30 minutes

I came to appreciate Brussels sprouts late in life. It's only been about 10 years since I started eating and preparing them. A friend who's a chef at a catering hall in the Bronx turned me on to them and to this wonderful recipe, to which I've made my own adjustments. To me, bacon can make just about anything taste great! So don't skimp on it here.

Tips to make it great:

Cook the bacon until crispy.

This dish often tastes better the next day, so it's not a bad idea to prepare the day before you want to serve it.

INGREDIENTS

1 pound Brussels sprouts

1/2 pound boneless chicken, cut into small cubes

2 tablespoons extra-virgin olive oil

1/2 teaspoon Himalayan pink salt

1/4 teaspoon black pepper

6 slices bacon

INSTRUCTIONS

1   Preheat the oven to 400 degrees F.

2   Trim the Brussels sprouts, then halve them, rinse, and pat dry.

3   Place the Brussels sprouts and chicken in a bowl and mix in the olive oil, salt, and pepper.

4   Line a large baking sheet with parchment paper.

5   Place the seasoned Brussels sprouts and chicken onto the lined baking sheet and bake for 25 minutes.

6   Place the bacon in a frying pan over medium-high heat and cook until crispy. Once cooked, crumble the bacon into small pieces. Transfer the baked chicken and Brussels sprouts to a large bowl, add the bacon, mix well, and serve.

TAVUK GÖĞSÜ (TURKISH CHICKEN BREAD PUDDING)

Serves 8 to 10

Prep Time: 10 minutes • Cook Time: 45 minutes

This is a famous Turkish dessert that I enjoyed immensely while visiting Istanbul, Turkey. I was truly surprised at how creamy and delicious this chicken-based dessert tasted. It's a fun recipe to prepare, too. I love turning people on to it.

Tips to make it great:

If possible, make this recipe the day before you need it. It must be refrigerated for at least two hours before eating, so making a day ahead is an advantage.

Use fresh chicken—not previously frozen.

Serve with vanilla ice cream or whipped cream.

INGREDIENTS

1/2 skinless boneless chicken breast

2/3 cup rice flour (you can substitute all-purpose flour, if necessary)

1/3 cup wheat starch (you can order wheat starch online or, if needed in a pinch, substitute with corn starch, but the flavor and outcome won't be quite the same)

5 cups whole milk, divided

1 cup granulated sugar

1 teaspoon vanilla extract

1 teaspoon ground cinnamon

INSTRUCTIONS

1 Wash the chicken breast thoroughly by running cold water over it for 5 minutes. Pat dry. Ensure that any smell from the chicken is gone. If it isn't, run the chicken under the water again or soak it in a bowl of water.

2 Fill a small pot with water, add the chicken, and bring to a boil. Once the water is boiling, lower the heat and allow the chicken to simmer for 25 minutes. Make sure the chicken is fully cooked. Squeeze all the water from the chicken and then set it aside to dry. Shred the chicken into fine pieces (put it into a blender or food processor or use a fork).

3   In a bowl, thoroughly mix the rice flour and wheat starch with 1 cup of the milk.

4   In a medium pot over medium-low heat, add the remaining 4 cups of milk. Slowly add the rice flour and wheat starch mixture to the pot and keep mixing as the contents turn to pudding. While still heating the mixture on low, spoon out a few tablespoons and add it to the shredded chicken to slightly warm it.

5   Slowly add all the chicken to the pot. Keep mixing vigorously. Add the sugar and cook over low heat until the sugar has dissolved. Remove the pot from the heat and add the vanilla extract.

6   Pour the contents of the pot into a glass pan and shake the cinnamon on top. Refrigerate for at least 2 hours. When ready to serve, use a spatula to cut small squares and place them on plates.

9

Emmy's Cucina

The Craigsmopolitan
The André
Traditional and Seafood Crostini
Grilled Octopus
Emmy's Watermelon and Goat Cheese Salad
Surf and Turf
Grilled Baby Asparagus
Affogato

1 am blessed to be writing this chapter while sitting on a terrace in Positano, Italy, south of Naples, overlooking the Tyrrhenian Sea. It is the final trip of my amazing sabbatical before I return to the faculty of Fordham's Gabelli School of Business. I have set my tomato timer (page 54) to be sure I complete my planned cookbook assignment for today, but also so I don't get so engrossed in it that I miss the beauty of this gorgeous green-blue sea before me.

This region of Italy is known for several special and beautiful ingredients: lemons, eggplant, zucchini, and tomatoes. You've already encountered many of my recipes featuring them, and now I'll share a few more in this chapter.

Among the many lessons I've learned during my 36-year career in academia, 10 years as a mutual fund director, and 39 years of marriage, three stand out that apply to my personal and professional life: loving (both yourself and others); listening with the intent to really learn; and being grateful for the small and large blessings in your life. For me, food—preparing it, sharing it, and eating it—has been the best teacher of how to love, how to listen, and how to be grateful.

In our family, food is a way to one's heart. It's our way of making someone feel truly and deeply loved. Through the years, I have learned that a good meal can greatly change a person's mood and actions. The "good meal effect" is something I've experienced in a multitude of settings, both at work and with my family.

The right dish at the right time has transformed many a "hangry" mood (a hunger that turned into anger), setting the stage for relaxed, meaningful conversation. In my professional life, I recall a colleague who headed the Executive MBA program reminding me about the importance of the weekend program's food budget. He regularly said, "When the food is good, everything else seems better, especially the quality of the program."

Beyond magical changes to mood and demeanor, sharing a good meal with someone builds what social psychologists call social capital: the presence of networks, relationships, shared norms, and trust among individuals and teams. Research shows that the benefits of social capital include low employee turnover, improved individual and team performance, greater innovation, and increased career mobility. There are numerous ways to build social capital in an organization, but from my perspective, one of the easiest ways is to invite colleagues to enjoy meals together. I have observed how casual mealtime conversation about non-work topics has greatly improved creativity and productivity.

As dean of the Gabelli School, I began to tie my demonstration of gratitude to food-related gifts. I would share recipes and brief anecdotes with my team at Christmas, along with a small cooking-related item with the school's logo on it that people could use in their own kitchens. One year, it was my recipe for Tiramisu (page 164) tucked into an espresso cup; another year, it was my family's recipe for Sunday Gravy (page 60) along with a Gabelli School apron. This was my way of sharing my love of food with my colleagues in the hope that they, in turn, would share their love with their friends and colleagues.

I received many notes letting me know that they "made my soup" or "tried my recipe." One colleague proudly collected all the gifts I'd given her over the years and sent me a photo of them being used on her holiday table. That brought me great joy for two reasons: first, that she was enjoying the gifts, and second, that she was thoughtful enough to send me the photo.

Showing love, listening, and demonstrating gratitude are all interrelated. At the Gabelli School, we used to hold an annual all-staff day, which was typically all about professional development. But after we did Chester Elton's motivators assessment (see page 85), I learned that the vast majority of the 80-person group valued having fun at work. In the years that followed, I gradually blended more fun with the professional development until we reached the right balance, with the desired outcome being learning while having a good time (if you can consider bowling a good time). We had many wonderful sessions, including one where we made costumes for story time at the children's hospital and another where we all became mixologists and made cocktails for ourselves.

I found ways to incorporate expressions of gratitude for one another, too. An activity that still stands out involved handing out blank stationery and pens. We asked everyone to think about three colleagues they'd like to thank, and we gave them time to write a brief note of appreciation. We then collected them, made sure that every employee had at least one special note, and delivered them. It seemed to create lasting joy and goodwill among the team.

While our note-writing exercise is an example of a successful organized effort, I can't stress enough that appreciation doesn't have to be choreographed. I have one faculty colleague who, to this day, emails me on every holiday—just a few words wishing me a happy Mother's Day or Happy New Year. The gesture means the world to me and reminds me, especially in difficult times, that my care for my colleagues was recognized and appreciated.

I have also used food to smoothe and soothe. Once, I spontaneously prepared my Tiramisu (see page 164 for recipe) for a colleague I was not seeing eye to eye with, and I believe our relationship improved after that. I made Sunday Gravy for a colleague in a nursing home who complained about the food, and Chicken Soup for the university's then-president when I learned he had a cold. Each of those acts helped me connect with the recipients in new ways.

Whether it's a holiday celebration, a summer barbeque, or a birthday dinner, the extra attention and love that goes into the food I prepare is repaid a thousand-fold by the feeling of satisfaction I get when people enjoy themselves at my table. As you may have noticed, ingredients are key to my approach to cooking. I believe that the recipe itself is only as good as the quality of the ingredients. Much like in business, the process might be good, but if the quality of the material isn't, the outcome won't be good either.

It may seem strange to mention a global pandemic in a book about food, but there's an important reason I will do so in this chapter. When COVID-19 arrived in the United States in the first quarter of 2020, the virus sent us indoors and into isolation to an extent that most of us had never experienced. Living in the New York area, where the virus hit hard at first was particularly difficult. Our children were worried about my and my husband's health and "didn't allow" us to go out of our home. I was working seven days a week, more than 12 hours a day, on Zoom. The video calls and the stress were relentless, and there was the potential for home to feel less like a refuge and more like a prison.

The place where my husband and I were trapped indoors was our summer home in Westhampton, New York, two hours east of Manhattan. We bought the house in 2013, a time of great difficulty followed by great relief. That was the year I was diagnosed with breast cancer and went through surgery and radiation treatment, and it was also the year my husband spent a month in the cardiac care unit of Columbia Presbyterian Hospital and suffered several near-death experiences. Both of us recovered, bringing a wave of relief to us and those around us.

The Westhampton house, which we call our "Happy Place," spoke to that relief. It became a source of great joy and many amazing celebrations, from an engagement party to a Kentucky Derby party (the horse we picked, Authentic, won that year!), and many barbeques.

During those early months of Covid-19, we were thrilled to hear that our daughters, Diana and Danielle, planned to join us in Westhampton for the weekend. In-person contact was in short supply, and they were among the people I most wanted to see. It would have been more than enough to simply spend time with them, but they brought a special treat I hadn't seen coming: they turned a small area off our kitchen into "Emmy's Cucina," a restaurant-like space named after our three-month-old granddaughter, Emmy.

In collaboration with Diana's husband, Craig, they prepared a wonderful meal. Danielle's husband, Andrew, was the waiter. Our son, James, and his wife, Jackie, couldn't join us, so when Andrew brought over the first cocktail, he honored them by saying that the first drink was on them. It was a fantastic meal and the next morning, while all the challenges of the pandemic remained, Emmy's Cucina had healed our souls.

Throughout this book, I've shared lessons about life and leadership that ingredients and recipes have brought to life for me, including the importance of gratitude, positivity, curiosity, persistence, humor, and embracing change. I encourage you to look for opportunities in your personal and professional life to use food and some of these lessons to connect with the people around you. I hope that food is a pathway to peace and joy for you and your family and friends, as it is for me. That's amore.

———————

This menu is based on the meal our children served us at the pop-up restaurant they named Emmy's Cucina on July 1, 2020. The menu they prepared was printed up for us, and I will always treasure it along with the memories from that very special evening.

THE CRAIGSMOPOLITAN

Makes 1 cocktail

Prep Time: 5 minutes

Our cooks creatively named a few of the menu items after themselves. This one is named after my son-in-law and the name is also, of course, a play on one of my favorite drinks, the Cosmopolitan.

Tips to make it great:

Serve in a chilled martini glass.

Use a lot of fresh lime. More lime creates more froth.

Cointreau is a must, and I use Grey Goose vodka.

INGREDIENTS

1 ounce Cointreau

2 ounces vodka

1 ounce cranberry juice

1 lime, divided

1 orange twist

INSTRUCTIONS

1 Put the Cointreau, vodka, and cranberry juice into a shaker filled with ice. Squeeze half the lime into the shaker and reserve the other half for garnish.

2 Shake all the ingredients well (ideally, some of the ice will chip off into the liquid). Using a strainer, pour the drink into chilled martini glass. Garnish with a slice of the remaining lime and drop the orange twist in the glass.

THE ANDRÉ

Makes 1 cocktail

Prep Time: 1 minute

My son-in-law, Andrew, is the namesake for this cocktail, an upscale version of my husband's go-to summer drink.

Tips to make it great:

> Serve in a rocks glass.
>
> Use large ice cubes and fresh grapefruit.
>
> Try Stolichnaya Elit vodka.

INGREDIENTS

3 ounces vodka

1 ounce freshly squeezed grapefruit juice

1 slice of lime

INSTRUCTIONS

1. Place two or three large, dense ice cubes into a rocks glass. Pour the vodka over the ice and add the grapefruit juice. Squeeze the slice of lime in, then drop the squeezed wedge into the glass and serve.

TRADITIONAL AND SEAFOOD CROSTINI

Serves 2

Prep Time: 20 minutes

Cook Time: 5 minutes

My son-in-law Andrew's family kindly shares their imported olive oil from Sicily with us, and this is one dish we always use their "liquid gold" on.

Tips to make it great:

Use French bread that is not too wide and slice it thin.

For the traditional crostini, use farm-fresh tomatoes and extra-virgin olive oil.

For the seafood crostini, use fresh crab meat and very ripe avocado.

For both types of crostini

1 Preheat the oven to 450 degrees F.

2 Put 2 tablespoons of the olive oil in a small bowl. Brush the oil on both sides of all 8 pieces of the bread and toast the slices on a baking sheet in the oven for 5 minutes, flipping the bread halfway through.

(continued on next page)

INGREDIENTS

For the traditional crostini

4 thin slices of French bread

1/4 cup extra-virgin olive oil, divided

1 large tomato, finely chopped

1 teaspoon Himalayan pink salt

Black pepper, to taste

1 basil leaf, finely chopped

For the seafood crostini

4 thin slices of French bread

1/4 cup extra-virgin olive oil, divided

1/2 avocado

Dash of Himalayan pink salt

1/2 cup jumbo lump crab meat

1/2 lemon

1 sprig of fresh parsley, chopped

INSTRUCTIONS

1   Chop the tomatoes very finely. Add the remaining 2 tablespoons of olive oil, salt, and pepper and mix well.

2   Using a spoon, cover the 4 pieces of toasted bread with the tomato mixture and then sprinkle with the chopped basil.

1   Mash the avocado and sprinkle with salt. Mix in the crab and the remaining 2 tablespoons of olive oil. Squeeze in the juice of the halved lemon and mix until the crab and avocado are combined.

2   Using a spoon, cover the 4 pieces of toasted bread with the crab mixture and then sprinkle with chopped parsley.

GRILLED OCTOPUS

Serves 2

Active Prep Time: 15 minutes, plus overnight marinating, or marinating for at least 2 hours

Cook Time: 80 minutes total: 45 minutes for boiling octopus,

25 minutes for potatoes, and 10 minutes for grilling octopus

Serve this as an entrée or as an appetizer and please, please enjoy it all year round! While it may seem a bit scary to prepare, I highly encourage you to take the risk. It's incredibly delicious and also low in fat and rich in protein.

Tips to make it great:

> Marinate the octopus overnight.
>
> Twice-cook it for tenderness.

I like to prepare this the night before I serve it, but you can do it in the morning as well.

INGREDIENTS

3 1/2 pound whole octopus (sold frozen in a fish market or delicacy shop)

4 fingerling potatoes

1 tablespoon Himalayan pink salt, plus a pinch more for seasoning the octopus

1/2 teaspoon ground black pepper, plus a pinch more for seasoning the octopus

1/4 cup extra-virgin olive oil for marinating, plus 2 tablespoons for the chickpea puree and 2 tablespoons for the potatoes

INSTRUCTIONS

1   Defrost the whole octopus. Fill a large pot with water and bring to a boil. Place the octopus in the boiling water and boil it for 45 minutes. Remove the octopus from the pot. Cut off the tentacles and place them in a bowl; discard the rest. (Alternatively, you can serve the octopus head after removing the ink pouch or save it to make fish stock.)

2   You will likely have more than 2 servings of tentacles, so you can save half covered in the refrigerator for a second meal later in the week, or you can re-freeze them for up to 1 month once they are boiled.

(continued on next page)

INGREDIENTS (cont.)

1/2 6-ounce jar of Kalamata olives

1 15.5-ounce can of chickpeas (you can use uncooked chickpeas, but they would require overnight soaking before boiling)

1/4 teaspoon garlic powder

1/2 lemon, for finishing

INSTRUCTIONS (cont.)

3   Marinate the boiled tentacles in pinch of salt, pinch of pepper, and 1/4 cup of olive oil, then refrigerate overnight, or for at least 2 hours.

4   The octopus needs to be at room temperature before grilling, so remove it from the refrigerator about 2 hours before you plan to grill and serve it.

5   Make the potatoes, which take the longest. Heat the grill to 375 degrees F. Prepare the potatoes by washing, quartering, and tossing them in a bowl with olive oil, salt, and pepper.

6   Put the potatoes on an aluminum foil-topped tray or baking sheet. Put the tray onto the grill for 15 minutes; stir and then cook for another 10 minutes. (You can also use an oven for the cooking step; bake at 375 degrees F for 25 minutes, turning after 12 minutes.) Remove the cooked potatoes and place them in a large bowl. Add the Kalamata olives and mix together. Set the bowl aside until the octopus is grilled.

7   Just before you plan to serve, turn the grill to medium-high and grill the octopus for 3 to 4 minutes. Turn it over and grill for 3 to 4 more minutes. Remove the tentacles from the grill and cut them into bite-sized pieces. Put the pieces in the bowl with the potatoes and olives.

8   Drain the chickpeas and season with garlic powder. Add a tablespoon of olive oil and mash or process to create a puree. If the consistency is not creamy, add a little water.

9   To plate, spoon the chickpea puree onto a dish, then spoon out the mixture of grilled octopus, potatoes, and olives. Finish with a squeeze of lemon.

EMMY'S WATERMELON AND GOAT CHEESE SALAD

Serves 2

Prep Time: 5 minutes

You're going to love this super-simple and delicious summer salad, especially when the watermelon is in season and bursting with flavor.

Tips to make it great:

Keep the watermelon chilled.

Use crumbled goat cheese.

INGREDIENTS

1/4 watermelon, cut into small chunks

8 ounces crumbled goat cheese

1/4 cup extra-virgin olive oil

1/4 cup balsamic vinegar

INSTRUCTIONS

1   Place the watermelon chunks in a large bowl. Add the goat cheese, oil, and vinegar, and mix thoroughly.

2   Chill for 15 minutes in the refrigerator before serving.

SURF AND TURF

Serves 2

Prep Time: 20 minutes • Cook Time: 20 minutes

This entrée will impress your guests and also looks beautiful on the plate. I like to prepare this when I'm hosting a small dinner party. Unlike a whole lobster, which I'm not able to cook (we all have our limits), I have no problem preparing these lobster tails.

Tips to make it great:

Baste the lobster tail with butter (I suggest the Kerrygold brand).

Try using a bone-in filet mignon and serve rare, using the reverse-sear approach explained in this recipe.

Be sure the meat and lobster are at room temperature before cooking.

INGREDIENTS

2 10-ounce bone-in filets (steak should be at least 1 1/2 inches thick)

2 5-ounce lobster tails

1 tablespoon Himalayan pink salt

1 teaspoon black pepper

1/2 stick butter, sliced

2 tablespoons lemon zest

1 lemon

1 teaspoon garlic powder

INSTRUCTIONS

1   Remove steak and lobster tails from the refrigerator 45 to 60 minutes before cooking so that they can come to room temperature.

2   To use a reverse-sear method — which slow-cooks meats at the beginning and then sears them on the hot grill to finish — start by preheating your grill to 275 degrees F.

3   Season the steaks with salt, pepper, and garlic powder. Transfer them to a metal rack and place them on the grill but not directly over the heat/flame. The easiest way to do this is by heating the right side of the grill and putting the rack with the steaks on the left side.

4   Insert a meat thermometer and close the grill for 45 to 60 minutes or until the meat reaches 110 degrees (you could also do this same process in the oven). Take the steaks off the grill and let them rest in foil for 10 minutes.

5   While the steak rests, cook the lobster tails.

6   Cut open the lobster tails and insert a few slices of butter into each. Sprinkle the lemon zest over the top. Wrap the tails in aluminum foil and grill for 5 minutes over medium heat.

7   Once the lobster is cooked, remove it from the grill and set it aside wrapped in foil until ready to serve. Before serving, squeeze the lemon over the top.

8   To finish the steaks, turn the grill up high. Sear each steak for one minute per side. Serve immediately with the lobster tails and the asparagus from the following recipe.

GRILLED BABY ASPARAGUS

Serves 2 to 4

Prep Time: 5 minutes

Cook Time: 3 to 4 minutes

At Emmy's Cucina, the steak and lobster tail from the preceding recipe were served on one large plate with this simple and extremely tasty asparagus.

INGREDIENTS

1 pound asparagus, trimmed

1 teaspoon Himalayan pink salt

1 teaspoon garlic powder

2 tablespoons extra-virgin olive oil

1/2 cup shaved Parmigiano-Reggiano

INSTRUCTIONS

1   Season the asparagus with the salt and garlic powder. Put a grill pan onto the stove over high heat and cook for 3 to 4 minutes.

2   Remove from the heat, shave the Parmigiano over the top, and serve.

AFFOGATO

Serves 2

Prep Time: 5 minutes

The first time we had affogato was more than 40 years ago at Ferrara's Bakery in lower Manhattan. It's a wonderful dessert we regularly make at home now and enjoy year round.

Tips to make it great:

> Use Illy coffee.
>
> Use your favorite ice cream flavor (we use vanilla).
>
> Use a glass serving cup.

INGREDIENTS

6 ounces espresso coffee

2 scoops ice cream

INSTRUCTIONS

1 You can make a large pot of espresso and serve the rest to drink. You can also use a Nespresso machine if you are only making a few servings. Once the espresso is made, scoop the ice cream into a glass or ceramic cup. Pour the hot espresso over the ice cream and enjoy immediately.

AFTER-DINNER CHEESE SELECTION

As you learned in the chapter on cheese, I am a cheese lover. When dining out, I often choose a cheese plate for dessert. The aroma of some of our selections has been known to cause some of our dining companions to grumble, "What is wrong with them?!" At one dinner, my brother even tried to block the smell by building a wall out of plates and napkins. At Emmy's Cucina, we all embraced the amazing array of aromas and delightful flavors of cheese. That night, they served us a mix of soft and hard cheeses—Romano, extra-aged gouda, Danish blue cheese, triple crème Brie, and cave-aged Gruyere—along with figs. Dreamy.

EPILOGUE

Compliments
of the Chef:
Holiday
Recipes

When I prepare for a holiday—any holiday—I start by making a menu, similar to how I've structured the recipes in each chapter of this book. I think about drinks to serve, appetizers to pass, a pasta, a main course, and of course, dessert.

Once I have my menu sketched out, it typically changes a bit as I learn who can and cannot join us. After I know who all our guests will be, I make a list of what I need from the various stores I'll shop at. I usually get the cold antipasto items from Casa Della Mozzarella and meat from Vincent's Meat Market. I go to Teitel Brothers for Pomi tomatoes, De Cecco pasta, and olive oil, and I buy most of my fish at Eastchester Fish Market in Westchester, with the exception of crab—for that, Randazzo's is my go-to! I set aside one day for shopping and one day for cooking, a beloved ritual that, year after year, adds up to a lifetime of stories and memories.

Holidays are a special time to show our love for one another through the festive and traditional foods and drinks we share as a family. The following recipes demonstrate the central nature of holidays to me—the ones I simply couldn't complete this cookbook without passing along to you. (To include *all* of my holiday recipes, well, I'd need another cookbook, so stay tuned.)

In my opinion, any day can feel like a holiday if you prepare the right meal. The recipes here are all attributed to particular days and holidays (and yes, the Super Bowl is a holiday in our house!), but the truth is that you can mix and match them all to your heart's desire. Maybe you want to turn a random Wednesday into a holiday. And why not? You only get one life, so you should definitely enjoy it!

NEW YEAR'S DAY

Festive Champagne Cocktail

Makes 1 cocktail

Prep Time: 5 minutes

I started making this special fizzy cocktail about 15 years ago. It's been such a winner that I shared it with my colleagues at Fordham along with a Gabelli School champagne glass. I enjoy either this cocktail or a "Craigsmopolitan" before my guests arrive for a holiday meal.

Tips to make it great:

> Use a chilled champagne glass.
>
> Use Korbel champagne.

INGREDIENTS

Half a fresh lime, divided

1 ounce Cointreau

1 ounce cranberry juice

6 ounces chilled champagne

INSTRUCTIONS

1   Squeeze 1 lime wedge into the chilled champagne glass. Pour in the Cointreau and then the cranberry juice. Fill the rest of the glass with the champagne (Korbel is my holiday entertaining favorite) and place the remaining lime wedge on the rim. Cheers!

Pigs in a Blanket

Serves 6

Prep Time: 10 minutes • Cook Time: 12 minutes

For me, it's not a holiday without pigs in a blanket. You may think it's okay to buy these already prepared in the frozen section of the supermarket, but if you do, you are seriously missing out. For 30-plus years, I've wrapped hot dogs in triangular Pillsbury dinner-roll dough and cut them into pieces, and it's been well worth it. On a recent Thanksgiving, my son-in-law Craig came up with an innovation: to cut the hot dogs and the dough into small pieces first. The resulting pigs in the blanket were even plumper and more delicious!

Tips to make it great:

> Use Hebrew National hot dogs.
>
> Use Pillsbury crescent rolls.
>
> Add sesame seeds for elegance.

INGREDIENTS

Cooking oil spray, for greasing

1 package hot dogs

1 package crescent roll–style dough

1/4 cup sesame seeds

INSTRUCTIONS

1 Preheat the oven to 375 degrees F.

2 Spray a baking sheet with cooking oil spray.

3 If you are in a hurry, roll each entire hot dog in one Pillsbury dough triangle and then cut each into 5 pieces. If you have more time, cut the hot dogs and the dough into 5 pieces each and then roll each piece separately. Sprinkle sesame seeds onto the dough for a more festive and finished look. Place the pieces on the baking sheet and bake for 12 minutes. Enjoy while still hot and provide some mustard for dipping.

Lentil Soup

Serves 6 to 8

Prep Time: 20 minutes • Cook Time: 1 hour

I simmer up big batches of this soup up all year long, but it's a tradition in Italian families to have at least one taste of lentils on New Year's Day to ensure good health for the whole year.

Beans will always have a special place in my heart, because for me, they reinforce the importance of having a sense of humor and the fact that you can only push people so far. As I mentioned in the introduction of this book, as a child I lived in a three-family house with my mom's brother and his wife. Uncle Tommy and Aunt Pat were a young couple, and I was, well, an annoying kid. I enjoyed spending time with them, and I suspect I overstayed my welcome on more than one occasion. My uncle would sometimes threaten me by saying, "If you don't behave, I'm going to shake the beans out of you." Of course, I didn't believe there would ever *really* be any repercussions.

But one day my uncle did, in fact, reach his limit on patience. He started shaking me while dropping beans on the floor, perhaps from his pocket (I think they may have been lentils). I remember crying, "My beans! I need my beans!" All the adults in the room found it hysterically funny. That was the first time I remember realizing that actions always have reactions. My mother's loving hug afterward reminded me that I wasn't all bad. To this day, I need my beans!

Tips to make it great:

> Use fresh lentils.
>
> Add pancetta or prosciutto.

INGREDIENTS

1 16-ounce bag of lentils

1/4 cup extra-virgin olive oil

4 garlic cloves, pressed or minced

1 medium yellow or white onion, chopped

2 carrots, peeled and chopped

1/4 cup diced prosciutto or pancetta (optional)

6 cups vegetable broth

2 cups water

1 teaspoon Himalayan pink salt, plus additional to taste

Freshly ground black pepper

1/2 pound small shell pasta (I recommend De Cecco conchigliette piccole #52)

Parmigiano-Reggiano (optional)

INSTRUCTIONS

1 Open the bag of lentils and pour them out on your countertop or tabletop. Sift through them by hand to remove any small pebbles or sticks. Then, rinse them in a colander and pat them dry.

2 Heat the olive oil in a 10- to 12-quart pot or Dutch oven over medium heat. When the oil is hot, add the garlic, onion, carrot, and prosciutto (optional), and cook, stirring often, about 5 minutes, until all ingredients are lightly browned.

3 Add the lentils, broth, water, salt, and pepper. Raise the heat and bring it to a boil for 10 minutes. After this, partially cover the pot and reduce the heat to maintain a gentle simmer. Cook for 30 to 40 additional minutes, or until the lentils are tender but still hold their shape.

4 Boil the pasta in a large pot of salted water, then drain and add it to the soup right before serving. Top the bowls of soup with grated Parmigiano-Reggiano to taste, if desired. If you have extra soup, you can freeze it before adding the pasta.

Rabbit Cacciatore

Serves 4 to 6

Prep Time: 20 minutes

Cook Time: 100 minutes (10 minutes for braising, 90 minutes for cooking)

This, along with my Lentil Soup (page 144), is always a huge part of our New Year's Day meal. This is one time when you shouldn't have too much trouble convincing someone that "it's chicken."

Tips to make it great:

Season the rabbit before browning.

For the wine, use Chianti (Peppoli is my go-to) or Cabernet Sauvignon.

Have patience and let it cook—it's just about impossible to overcook it.

INGREDIENTS

1 red bell pepper, sliced into very thin strips

1/3 cup onion, sliced very thin

1 cup baby portobello mushrooms, sliced very thin

4 Yukon Gold potatoes

1 (4 to 5 pound) rabbit (ask the butcher to cut it into 8 pieces)

1 teaspoon Himalayan pink salt, plus more for seasoning the sauce

1/2 teaspoon black pepper, plus more for seasoning the sauce

INSTRUCTIONS

1 Cut the peppers, onion, and mushrooms as previously noted. Peel the potatoes and chop them into bite-sized pieces.

2 Wash the rabbit and pat it dry. Season it with the salt, pepper, and garlic powder. In a large, nonstick frying pan over medium heat, add 2 tablespoons of the extra virgin olive oil. Add 1 1/2 teaspoons of the garlic. Brown the rabbit pieces with the garlic on both sides. Once browned, transfer them to a paper towel-lined plate.

3 Using the same pan, add the red peppers and then, as they soften, the mushrooms and onion. Once the peppers, mushrooms, and onions are lightly browned, transfer them to a bowl and set aside.

INGREDIENTS (cont.)

1 teaspoon garlic powder

1/4 cup extra-virgin olive oil, divided

1 tablespoon chopped garlic, divided

1/4 cup red wine

2 26-ounce boxes strained Pomi tomatoes

Sprig of parsley

INSTRUCTIONS (cont.)

4   In an 8-quart pot over medium-high heat, add the remaining 2 tablespoons of olive oil and the remaining half-teaspoon of chopped garlic. Add the rabbit, peppers, mushrooms, and onions into the pot. Then add the wine and tomatoes. Next, add the potatoes and parsley, then salt and pepper to taste. Stir everything using a wooden spoon.

5   Bring the sauce to a boil for 5 minutes, then lower it to a simmer and stir frequently for 80 minutes. The potatoes should be soft, and the rabbit will be very tender by the end, almost falling off the bone.

6   Transfer the rabbit to a flat serving platter covered with the peppers, potatoes, mushrooms, onion, and sauce.

Stuffed Artichokes

Serves 3 to 4

Prep Time: 20 minutes • Cook Time: 40 minutes

Traditionally, my grandmother would make stuffed artichokes for holidays, complaining about how much each artichoke costs but buying them anyway. She would cut the tips off with scissors and stuff each leaf with a mix of seasoned breadcrumbs and olive oil. I will never forget the sound of her banging each and every artichoke on the table to ensure they were fully stuffed with the delicious filling. Though I make these often, I never make them quite as well as she did (but then again, I don't think anyone could).

Tips to make it great:

Stuff them fully, but don't overstuff.

Keep spooning the liquid in the pot of the artichokes.

Serve with extra-virgin olive oil and red wine vinegar for dipping.

INGREDIENTS

3 large artichokes

1 cup 4C Seasoned Breadcrumbs (or homemade or another brand)

3 tablespoons grated Parmigiano-Reggiano

1 carrot

1 celery stalk

1 small onion

2 to 3 cups water

1 chicken bouillon cube

3 tablespoons extra-virgin olive oil, divided

INSTRUCTIONS

1   Wash and dry the artichokes. Trim them with scissors, cutting all the tips straight. Bang the artichokes face down on the table to open them.

2   In a small bowl, mix the breadcrumbs and Parmigiano.

3   Stuff the artichokes with the breadcrumb-and-cheese mix by gently pulling back the leaves. Bend the artichokes face up to allow the mixture to settle in, then add more of the mix until each artichoke is stuffed full.

4   Finely dice the carrot, celery, and onion and place all of it into a pot with the water. Add the chicken bouillon and 2 tablespoons of the olive oil.

INSTRUCTIONS (cont.)

5   Carefully transfer the stuffed artichokes to the pot of water, setting them in it with the open tops facing up. They should be immersed more than halfway. Drizzle the tops of the artichokes lightly with the remaining 1 tablespoon of olive oil.

6   Over high heat, bring the water to a boil, then cover the pot and lower to a simmer. Simmer for 30 to 40 minutes. Every 10 minutes or so, uncover the pot, spoon the liquid in the pot over the artichokes, and then cover them again and continue cooking. Serve hot with additional olive oil and red wine vinegar for dipping.

Aunt Rita's Nut Cookies

Serves 12 to 16 (makes 36 cookies)
Prep Time: 20 minutes • Cook Time: 10 minutes

Making these cookies was a longtime family Christmas tradition. I would typically make so many that they lasted well into New Year's. That all stopped when we learned that one of our daughters was allergic to tree nuts. We've since been at the mercy of Aunt Rita to bake them for those of us who can safely enjoy them.

Preheat the oven to 400 degrees F.

INGREDIENTS

For the dough

1/2 pound cream cheese at room temperature

1/2 pound butter at room temperature

2 extra large egg yolks

2 1/2 cups all-purpose flour, plus more for dusting

1 teaspoon baking powder

For the filling

1/2 pound chopped walnuts

3/4 cup granulated sugar

Dash of cinnamon

Drop of whole milk

Powdered sugar

Cooking oil spray, for greasing

INSTRUCTIONS

1   In a large bowl, mix the cream cheese, butter, egg yolks, flour, and baking powder until fully incorporated. Lightly knead the dough on a flour-dusted surface and form 6 small balls. Flatten each portion of dough using a rolling pin to create an approximate circle that is about 9 inches in diameter. Then cut the circle into six triangles, as if you are cutting a pizza.

2   In a medium bowl, mix all of the filling ingredients together. The resulting mixture should be quite thick.

To form the cookies

1. Spoon a small amount of filling into the center of each dough triangle. Roll the triangle from the large end toward the point to capture the filling inside.

2. Place the rolls on a greased baking sheet and bake for 8 to 10 minutes. Sprinkle with powdered sugar after removing from the oven.

SUPER BOWL SUNDAY

Beefeater Gibson

Makes 1 cocktail

Prep Time: 5 minutes

From the late 1970s until his death in 2004, my father went with my uncle and their friends to the Super Bowl. They spent months planning those trips and then months after reminiscing about all the fun they had. My dad's favorite drink was a Beefeater Gibson. I try to make and enjoy one on his birthday every year, but they are pretty strong. In recent years, I only manage a sip or two.

Tips to make it great:

> Serve in a chilled martini glass.
>
> Prepare in a glass pitcher.
>
> Add extra onions.

INGREDIENTS

2 1/2 ounces Beefeater gin

1/2 ounce dry vermouth

3 or 4 cocktail onions

INSTRUCTIONS

1   Fill a small cocktail pitcher with ice. If you are going to prepare this drink often, I recommend investing in a tall, narrow glass pitcher with a glass stirrer, but any pitcher (or even a very tall glass) will do.

2   Fill whatever you've got with ice, and then add the gin and vermouth and stir for 1 minute. Using a strainer, pour your Gibson into a chilled martini glass, add your cocktail onions, and cheers!

Tostitos with Cheese

Serves 1 or 2

Prep Time: 5 minutes • Cook Time: 12 seconds

I am a bit embarrassed to share that if I could bring only one food item to a deserted island, it would be Tostitos. Not the scoops or the lime-flavored ones, but the original restaurant-style. I eat them at least once a week, and I've been known to prepare the recipe below as a meal for myself after a long day of work. More recently, I make them as a family snack, and they are, of course, a Super Bowl staple for us.

Tips to make it great:

> Use name-brand Tostitos and Land O Lakes yellow American cheese.
>
> Eat immediately!

INGREDIENTS

10 to 12 original restaurant-style Tostitos

5 slices American cheese

1/2 package onion soup mix

1/2 cup sour cream

INSTRUCTIONS

1   Line a large paper dish with the Tostitos. Halve the slices of cheese and cover as many of the Tostitos with the cheese as possible. Ideally, all of them will have some amount of cheese on them. Set aside.

2   Make the onion dip by thoroughly blending the soup mix and sour cream.

3   Once the onion dip is mixed, transfer the cheese-covered chips to the microwave and cook for 12 seconds. The cheese should be melted at this point. Using a spoon, layer dollops of onion dip on top of the melted cheese. I enjoy this snack with a glass of Jordan Cabernet Sauvignon, but others often prefer beer or soda with them.

Super Bowl Chili

Serves 10

Prep Time: 1 hour • Cook Time: 5 hours

Chili is a mainstay for this mid-winter, football-fueled holiday as well as many others. My husband generally makes this chili a few times a year and often doubles the recipe so that there's enough to stow some away in the freezer for another day.

Tips to make it great:

> Use high-fat-content beef.
>
> Season the meat as you cook it.
>
> Cook it for a very long time. This is a dish you can't overcook! Leave a wooden spoon in the pot while cooking so the chili doesn't burn.

INGREDIENTS

5 pounds high-fat-content ground beef

2 teaspoons Himalayan pink salt

2 teaspoons black pepper

1/4 cup plus 2 tablespoons extra-virgin oil, divided

3 medium onions, chopped

3 red bell peppers, seeded and chopped

5 garlic cloves, finely chopped

6 boxes Pomi chopped tomatoes

1 tablespoon plus 2 teaspoons chipotle chili powder

3 large (15.5-ounce) cans of kidney beans

INSTRUCTIONS

1   Season the beef with salt and pepper and then brown it in a large frying pan over medium-high heat with 1/4 cup of oil. Make sure the meat is thoroughly cooked. Transfer it to a very large pot.

2   Add the remaining oil to the frying pan. Brown the onion, red pepper, and garlic. Cook, stirring, until the onion and peppers are soft, and then transfer them to the large pot.

3   Add the tomato sauce, spices, and beans to the large pot. Bring everything in it to a boil over high heat, then reduce heat to a simmer and simmer for about 5 hours. Put a large wooden spoon in the pot as it cooks to keep the chili from burning. Keep tasting it and adding spices as needed throughout cooking.

EASTER SUNDAY

Espresso Martini

Makes 1 cocktail

Prep Time: 5 minutes

Espresso martinis are a family favorite, and although they can be served anytime during a meal, I think they're best at the end, as a little pick-me-up. I use a variety of flavored beans, and I love to put salted caramel espresso beans into the bottom of the glass when serving.

Tips to make it great:

> Chill the martini glass in the freezer for 15 minutes.
>
> I use Grey Goose vodka and Mr. Black coffee liqueur, but there are many brands to choose from.
>
> Make the coffee early in the day.
>
> Use plenty of ice.

INGREDIENTS

1.5 ounces vodka

1.5 ounces espresso

1 ounce coffee liqueur

2 coffee beans, for garnish

Orange zest, for garnish

INSTRUCTIONS

1. Pour the vodka, espresso, and coffee liqueur into a shaker filled with ice. Shake well.

2. Put the two coffee beans in the bottom of the chilled glass. Pour the chilled drink over the beans and garnish with the orange zest.

Stuffed Zucchini Flowers

Serves 4 to 6

Prep Time: 15 minutes • Cook Time: 10 minutes

I've enjoyed zucchini flowers for many years, but only after taking a recent cooking class in Italy did I learn how to prepare these stuffed and pan-fried *fiori di zucchine ripieni*. In New York, zucchini flowers are available at upscale grocery stores (I buy mine at DeCicco and Sons) and farmers markets from spring until fall, but I wish they were in season all year long!

Tips to make it great:

> Use the largest zucchini flowers you can find.
>
> Serve them on a bed of marinara sauce or Sunday Gravy (page 60).

INGREDIENTS

12 zucchini flowers

1 cup chopped mozzarella

2 cups ricotta

2 fresh basil leaves, chopped and divided

1/4 cup grated Parmigiano-Reggiano, plus more for topping

1/2 teaspoon Himalayan pink salt

Dash of black pepper

2 extra large eggs

1/2 cup Italian seasoned breadcrumbs

1/4 cup all-purpose flour

1/4 cup extra-virgin olive oil, for frying

INSTRUCTIONS

1 Gently rinse the zucchini flowers in cold water. Remove and discard the stems around the bottom of the flowers. Set the blossoms aside on a paper towel.

2 In a large bowl, prepare the filling by stirring together the mozzarella, ricotta, 1 of the chopped basil leaves, the Parmigiano-Reggiano, salt, and pepper. Mix well until everything is fully incorporated.

3 Gently open each zucchini flower from top to bottom so that they are all open and lying flat. Fill each flower, depending on its size, with 1 to 2 heaping tablespoons of the filling. They should be very full. Close the flowers by gently rolling them on the countertop and pinching both ends closed. Set them aside.

4   Beat the eggs in a large bowl. Pour the breadcrumbs evenly onto a flat dish.

5   One at a time, dip the stuffed flowers into the eggs and then roll them in the breadcrumbs.

6   Once all of the flowers are breaded, heat the olive oil in a large frying pan over medium heat. Fry the flowers until golden brown, about 5 to 7 minutes. Transfer them to a paper towel-lined plate to rest for 1 to 2 minutes.

7   For serving, nestle the flowers in a bed of Marinara Sauce (page 190) or Sunday Gravy (page 60). Sprinkle the remaining chopped basil and a little more Parmigiano over the top.

"Torta" (Potato Pie)

Serves 12 to 16 (2 pies)

Prep Time: 60 minutes

Bake Time: 45 minutes

This is my mother-in-law Angie's recipe. It's called *torta* in her Italian dialect, and it's been enjoyed by many people for many years, including my family! The first time I made this recipe, I was at Angie's home, and she tripled the recipe so that she'd have enough to give away for family and friends. Yes, the 15 pounds of potato peeling did seem endless. Below is a slightly more manageable approach. I promise you the outcome is well worth the effort. We enjoy it as an appetizer alongside a charcuterie board or as a delicious leftover.

Tips to make it great:

> Boil the potatoes in well-salted water.
>
> Use imported grated Pecorino Romano.
>
> Serve hot.

INGREDIENTS

For the filling

5 pounds Yukon Gold potatoes

1/4 cup iodized salt for the boiling water

4 extra large eggs, divided

1 tablespoon extra-virgin olive oil

1 cup chopped leeks

1 tablespoon garlic powder

1 tablespoon oregano

1 teaspoon Himalayan pink salt

1 teaspoon black pepper

1 1/2 pounds salted butter, plus extra for greasing the baking sheets

1 cup sour cream

2 cups grated Pecorino Romano

For the dough

2 cups all-purpose flour, plus more for dusting

2 teaspoons extra-virgin olive oil

1/2 teaspoon salt

2 extra large eggs

1/2 cup water, as needed

INSTRUCTIONS

1 Preheat the oven to 375 degrees F.

2 Fill a large pot with water and set it over high heat. Peel the potatoes, quarter them into wedges, and transfer them to the pot. Add the salt and boil the potatoes until they are tender. Strain them and transfer to a paper towel–lined platter to absorb the extra water.

3 Meanwhile, make the dough.

4 Generously grease 2 baking sheets with butter.

5 In a large bowl, combine all of your dough ingredients, adding the flour incrementally, and adding water as needed to soften the dough. Once the dough is well blended and can be shaped into 2 cohesive balls, dust a clean surface with flour and use a flour-dusted rolling pin to roll out each dough ball to just over the size of a large baking sheet.

6 Transfer each sheet of dough onto a greased baking sheet with the extra dough hanging over the side. Set aside.

7 Crack 3 of the eggs into a large bowl. Add the olive oil and salt, and mix. Set aside.

8 In a medium pan over medium heat, sauté the leek, garlic powder, oregano, salt, and pepper in butter. Transfer this mixture to a large pot and add the cooked potatoes, sour cream, grated cheese, and egg mix. Stir to fully incorporate and then set aside to cool to room temperature.

(continued on next page)

INSTRUCTIONS (cont.)

9 Once the mixture is cooled, use a large spoon to transfer it evenly onto the middle of the dough-lined baking sheets. Fold the excess dough over the top of the mixture and combine it at the top so that you seal the edges and fully enclose the tortas.

10 In a small bowl beat the remaining egg. Use a pastry brush to coat the top of each pie with the beaten egg and prick the top of the pie with a fork. Bake each pie for 45 minutes.

11 Let rest for 2 to 3 minutes before slicing and serving. You can freeze one or both of the tortas as soon as they have cooled. Just be sure to wrap tightly.

Bone-in Leg of Lamb

Serves 4 to 6

Prep Time: 10 minutes

Cook Time: 60 minutes for rare

Holidays weren't always easy for me. In the Introduction, I told you all about that first family holiday I hosted in Easter of 1985 when I ordered half a baby lamb. I was very excited to receive the delivery from the butcher until I opened the paper and saw the half lamb, sawed down the middle—eyeball and all! I closed the paper immediately and called my grandmother, who at the time lived just around the corner. She came and saved me, cleaning the lamb and cutting it for me so that I could roast it in my small oven.

My goal that day was to show my love and gratitude for my in-laws very early in my marriage—and it worked! My father-in-law thoroughly enjoyed the roast lamb. (I closed my eyes, so I can't totally be sure, but I think he even ate the eyeball.)

Eyeballs aside, roast lamb is truly a wonderful dish, assuming you can purchase the lamb already cleaned or have someone help you clean it. These days, I opt for bone-in leg of lamb, because well, it's a little easier.

Tips to make it great:

Let lamb rest out of the refrigerator for about 1 hour or until it's at room temperature.

Season the lamb well.

Do not overcook it! The lamb will continue to cook after you take it out of the oven, and there is no "uncooking" when it comes to meat.

(continued on next page)

INGREDIENTS

1 bone-in leg of lamb (5 to 7 pounds)

3 tablespoons extra-virgin olive oil

Himalayan pink salt and freshly ground black pepper, to taste

6 cloves of garlic, kept whole for rubbing on the meat

INSTRUCTIONS

1   Arrange your oven rack so that the top of the lamb will be a few inches from the broiler. Turn on the broiler.

2   Rinse the lamb and pat it dry. Let the lamb rest for 1 hour until it reaches room temperature. Transfer the lamb to a rack inside a roasting pan. Drizzle it with the olive oil and rub it in by hand, making sure that you coat all parts. Season it generously with the salt and pepper, making sure that you season all parts. Position the lamb on the rack in the pan so that it is fat-side down.

3   Place the lamb in the oven and broil each side for 5 minutes. After both sides have broiled and are browned, remove the lamb from the oven and rub it thoroughly with the garlic. Then, using toothpicks, place the garlic cloves on top of the lamb, piercing through the cloves into the flesh. Tent the lamb on the rack and pan with foil.

4   Turn off the broiler, and with oven mitts, reposition the rack so that it's in the middle of the oven.

5   Preheat the oven to 325 degrees F.

6   Roast the lamb for 1 hour. Remove it from the oven and, using a meat thermometer, take the temperature of the thickest part of the lamb. You want it to be 125 degrees F or above.

7   At this temperature it may look too rare, but it will continue cooking as it rests, so I recommend taking it out of the oven once it reaches 125 degrees F or higher. You can always cook it a little more after you carve into it. Let it rest for 10 minutes, then carve. If you still think it's too rare, return it to the oven to roast for another 15 minutes. Either way, let the lamb rest for 10 minutes before carving and serving.

Mom's Mashed Potatoes

Serves 4 to 6

Prep Time: 15 minutes • Cook Time: 20 minutes

My mom has always made delicious mashed potatoes. When I was growing up, our holiday table featured either pasta or potatoes, not both. My in-laws, however, always served both, and I got spoiled by that. Now I wouldn't think of hosting a holiday without potatoes and pasta alongside the meat.

Tips to make it great:

> Use very cold, salty water.
>
> Strain the potatoes well.
>
> Use heavy cream instead of milk.

INGREDIENTS

3 pounds Yukon Gold potatoes (5 to 6), peeled and cut into 1-inch cubes

1/4 cup Himalayan pink salt

1/4 cup iodized salt for the boiling water

4 cloves garlic (optional)

1/2 cup heavy cream

3/4 stick salted Kerrygold butter (or your butter of choice)

1/4 teaspoon black pepper

INSTRUCTIONS

1 Place the cut potatoes in a large pot and add enough cold water to cover them with an additional inch to spare. Add the salt and garlic. Bring the water to a boil over high heat, then reduce to a simmer, and simmer until the potatoes are fork-tender, about 10 minutes. Don't overcook, but also make sure the potatoes are no longer firm.

2 Drain the potatoes and return them to the pot. You can either leave the garlic in with the potatoes or discard it. Add the heavy cream, butter, salt, and pepper.

(continued on next page)

INSTRUCTIONS (cont.)

3   Using a hand mixer, blend all the mashed potatoes to the desired consistency and enjoy.

4   If you are making these ahead, you can transfer the mashed potatoes to a glass pan, add some small pats of butter to the top, and later bake them in the oven at 350 degrees F until warmed through before serving. Also, I highly recommend using any leftover potatoes to make potato croquettes.

Tiramisu

Serves 8 to 10

Prep Time: 20 minutes (plus 2 hours for refrigeration)

Cook Time: 10 minutes for espresso

Please note that this tiramisu is a friend-maker! My friend, Loretta, shared this recipe with me more than 25 years ago. Over those years, I've prepared it for scores of friends, as well as for some with whom I have hoped to be more friendly! I also taught this recipe during a special cooking class for my Fordham colleagues. It's simple, delicious, and you really can't mess it up.

Tips to make it great:

Use Illy or Lavazza espresso coffee.

If you have time, separate the eggs 30 minutes beforehand. They are easier to separate when cold, but the egg whites can be beaten to a fluffier consistency when you allow them to come to room temperature.

Use an egg separator. Any yolk at all will reduce the fluff-ability.

INGREDIENTS

8 to 10 cups espresso coffee

2 ounces Kahlua or amaretto (optional)

5 extra large eggs, yolks and whites divided

1/2 cup granulated sugar

1 pound mascarpone

40 Savoiardi ladyfingers

1 tablespoon cocoa powder

Chocolate shavings (optional)

INSTRUCTIONS

1 Make the espresso coffee and let it cool. Add the Kahlua or amaretto to the espresso, if you are using it. Depending on the size of your pot, you may need to make 2 batches to produce the amount you need.

2 Separate the eggs, adding the whites to a large bowl and the yolks to another.

3 With the egg yolks, mix in the sugar, and then fold in the mascarpone. Set aside.

4 Using an electric mixer, beat the egg whites until fluffy.

5 Combine the fluffy whites into the bowl with the yolks.

6 Choose a tray you'd like to make your tiramisu in. There are lots of options. You can use a square or rectangular pan, about 9 or 10 inches to a side; an aluminum pan; or individually sized portions in small cups.

7 If you use 1 large pan, dip 1 ladyfinger cookie at a time into the espresso coffee (with the Kahlua or amaretto, if added) and, as you go, layer the bottom of the pan with the moistened cookies. Once you've finished a full layer of espresso-dipped ladyfingers, spoon the mascarpone-egg mix on top. Repeat this process to create a second layer of cookies and mascarpone-egg mix.

8 If you are making individual cups, break each ladyfinger in half before dipping it into the coffee. Use the process described above until you've filled each individual cup.

9 For either, sprinkle the cocoa powder and chocolate shavings, if using, evenly over the top. Refrigerate for at least 2 hours before serving.

FOURTH OF JULY

As I mentioned, we spend a lot of time during the summer months in our home in West-hampton, New York. The one flaw in that home is the electric stove. I'm still trying to get used to it. I generally move my kitchen outside to the barbeque grill, which has a propane burner, to make my crab sauce and other dishes that need a more controlled flame. I was told by a wonderful chef that once I got used to my electric stove, I'd never want to use a flame again. It's a decade later, and well, I'm still waiting.

The recipes that follow are a sampling of what I like to serve at our summer barbeques, particularly the Fourth of July, but they can certainly be prepared year round.

Blackberry Mojito

Makes 1 cocktail

Prep Time: 5 minutes

The first time I had this mojito was on Paradise Island in the Bahamas, and it was love at first sip. My daughter-in-law, Jackie, makes it even better than any bartender in the Caribbean! You're going to really enjoy it.

Tips to make it great:

> Use plenty of ice.
>
> Use fresh mint and blackberries.
>
> I use Zacapa rum, but you can use any rum of your choosing.
>
> Serve in a tall, chilled glass.

INGREDIENTS

Fresh mint, for muddling and for garnish

5 blackberries

Fresh lime, for muddling and for garnish

2 ounces rum

Splash of club soda

INSTRUCTIONS

1 Muddle a handful of mint, the blackberries, and 2 slices of lime. Place the rum into a shaker with the muddled mixture. Add ice and shake thoroughly.

2 Pour and strain the cocktail into a tall, chilled glass filled with ice. Top with the club soda, and garnish with fresh mint and lime.

Tzatziki Dip

Serves 4 to 6

Prep Time: 15 minutes

I learned how to make this lemony, garlicky dip in Santorini, Greece, but I significantly improved my recipe based on a conversation with Mario Gabelli and his wife, Regina Pitaro, who turned me onto Siggi's, a brand of skyr Icelandic yogurt. I highly recommend serving it with a crudité or pita chips.

Tips to make it great:

If your cucumbers have big seeds, remove them.

Be generous with the extra-virgin olive oil.

INGREDIENTS

1 cucumber

1 1/2 cups Siggi's Icelandic skyr yogurt or fat-free plain Greek yogurt

2 tablespoons finely diced red onion

1 teaspoon Garlic Paste (see page 17)

2 tablespoons extra-virgin olive oil

1 teaspoon red wine vinegar

1 tablespoon fresh chopped dill

Juice and the zest of 1 lemon

Himalayan pink salt and freshly cracked black pepper, to taste

INSTRUCTIONS

1 Peel the cucumber. If the seeds are large, remove them before grating the cucumber with a cheese grater. Squeeze the excess water from the grated cucumber, discard it, and transfer the grated cucumber to a new bowl.

2 Add the yogurt, onion, and garlic paste to the cucumber and fluff with a fork. Fold in the olive oil, vinegar, dill, lemon juice, and zest, and season with salt and black pepper.

3 Add more olive oil if desired, as well as more salt and pepper, if needed. Enjoy right away or store in a sealed container in the refrigerator for up to 1 week.

String Bean, Tomato, and Potato Salad

Serves 10

Prep Time: 15 minutes

Cook Time: 20 minutes

I make this salad so often that my children have been known to tease me about it—pretending, or at least I think they are pretending, to be tired of it by lamenting, "Not the string bean salad again . . ."

Whether or not they're tired of it, I've shared the recipe with my colleagues at Fordham and they all seem to love it. As I note below, please watch the potatoes: I have on occasion both overcooked and undercooked them. As with everything, being attentive to the pot makes a world of difference.

Tips to make it great:

Use fresh string beans and fresh tomatoes.

Don't overcook the potatoes, but don't undercook them either.

Use extra-virgin olive oil.

(continued on next page)

INGREDIENTS

6 Yukon Gold potatoes

1 pound string beans

2 garlic cloves, peeled and finely chopped

1 16-ounce container of cherry tomatoes, quartered

1/4 cup finely chopped red onion

1/4 cup extra-virgin olive oil

1/4 cup balsamic vinegar

1 teaspoon Himalayan pink salt

1/4 cup iodized salt for the boiling water

Black pepper, to taste

INSTRUCTIONS

1   Peel the potatoes and cut them into bite-sized wedges. Fill a pot with water and place the potato pieces into it. Bring to a boil over high heat, then add the iodized salt.

2   Boil the potatoes for roughly 20 minutes, until cooked through. Keep a close watch on their progress by sticking them now and again with a fork. If you must lean one way or the other, it's better that they are underdone than overdone. Strain the cooked potatoes, run them under cold water, and set aside.

3   Wash and trim the ends of the string beans. In a large pot over high heat, add 1 cup of water along with the string beans, and cover. Boil them for about 10 minutes. You want them to still be fairly firm and bright green when done. Strain the beans, and run them under cold water to stop them from cooking.

4   Transfer the cooked and cooled potatoes and the cooked and cooled string beans to a large bowl. Stir in the garlic, tomatoes, red onion, oil, vinegar, salt, and pepper. Enjoy chilled.

Pasta Salad

Serves 8 to 20

Prep Time: 20 minutes • Cook Time: 20 minutes

I've made this pasta salad hundreds of times. It's a staple at all of our family barbeques, and I've also started making it a few times in the winter—it conjures up memories of summer when the days are short and cold. It's one of my son James's favorites. He has been known to eat the leftovers all week long.

Tips to make it great:

Mix in an extra-large tray.

Use two kinds of vinegar.

Let it sit for a few hours before serving.

(continued on next page)

INGREDIENTS

1/4 cup iodized salt

1 pound pasta (consider De Cecco fusilli #24 or farfalle #93)

1 16-ounce container of cherry tomatoes

12 ounces marinated artichoke hearts

8 small mozzarella balls or 4 large mozzarella balls

12 ounces jarred roasted red bell peppers

8 1/2 ounces sliced black pearl olives

3 tablespoons extra-virgin olive oil

2 teaspoons red wine vinegar

2 teaspoons balsamic vinegar

1 teaspoon Himalayan pink salt

1 teaspoon black pepper

INSTRUCTIONS

1   Fill a large pot with water and bring it to a boil over high heat. Once the water is boiling, add the iodized salt and pasta. Cook the pasta for 10 to 12 minutes. For this salad, you don't want the pasta fully cooked. Once the pasta is done, strain it and run under cold water for a few minutes until completely cooled. Set aside.

2   Halve the cherry tomatoes and transfer them to a large tray, approximately 13 by 21 inches. Slice the artichoke hearts, mozzarella, and roasted peppers into bite-sized pieces, and add them along with the olives to the tray. Stir everything together.

3   Add the cooked pasta, olive oil, vinegars, salt, and pepper. Stir to fully incorporate. Transfer the pasta salad to a large round bowl and refrigerate covered for at least 2 hours before serving.

Skirt Steak

Serves 6 to 8

Prep Time: 20 minutes (plus time in the refrigerator)

Cook Time: 10 to 15 minutes

In addition to hamburgers, hot dogs, and sausage on the grill, we serve skirt steak at just about every barbeque. Our son James does a great job not only creating a huge mess, but also preparing and cooking this barbeque mainstay.

At some point, I was surprised to discover how expensive skirt steak is. Was it a constraint of supply or demand? It turns out it's a bit of both, but mostly the former. Skirt steak comes from one of two separate muscles of the cow: the diaphragm muscle (the outside skirt), which is what most restaurants and commercial kitchens use, or the transversus abdominis muscle (the inside skirt), which is what individual consumers usually find in the butcher shop. Because the amount of skirt steak a cow yields is quite small, the cost is relatively high. Despite the high-ticket price, though, I splurge and serve it all summer long. It's a real crowd-pleaser.

Tips to make it great:

Prepare and marinate the steak overnight.

Cook at room temperature.

Make a big mess!

INGREDIENTS

5-pound skirt steak

2 bottles A.1. Original Sauce

1/4 cup garlic powder

2 cups apple cider vinegar

2 teaspoons Himalayan pink salt

2 teaspoons black pepper

INSTRUCTIONS

1   Marinate the steak the day before you cook it. Combine the A.1. Original Sauce, garlic powder, and vinegar in a metal tray (it can be a disposable aluminum pan) large enough to allow the steak to lie flat. Mix well and set aside.

2   Trim the white membrane and excess fat off the steak and discard it. Season the meat using 1 teaspoon each of the salt and pepper. Save the rest for just before serving.

3   Transfer the steak to the pan with the marinade. It's important that the steak be completely submerged. Cover and refrigerate it overnight.

4   About 3 or 4 hours before you plan to grill the steak, remove it from the refrigerator and let it come to room temperature.

5   With the grill set to medium, cook the steak for 5 minutes, flipping it once. Increase the flame and heat, and cook for an additional 2 1/2 minutes, flipping it once. Remove it from the grill, season with remaining salt, and let it cool for 5 minutes before serving. Slice the steak against the grain of the meat.

Seafood Paella

Serves 4 to 6

Prep Time: 60 minutes • Cook Time: 60 minutes

Our children enjoy trying new recipes, and summer is often a great time to experiment. Our daughter, Diana, bought us an outdoor paella pan that connects to a propane tank, and she led us in preparing seafood paella. This family experiment reinforced the importance of patience and teamwork when it comes to cooking. We've used our portable outdoor paella pan dozens of times now, and I highly suggest considering one if you have the space. This is a wonderful summer recipe.

Tips to make it great:

Gather a small group of family or friends and make this one together.

Be patient, as this dish requires you to pay attention to each and every step.

Use very large shrimp, 10 to 12 per pound.

Choose a wine for this that you would happily drink.

If needed, add more seafood stock.

INGREDIENTS

12 mussels

8 littleneck and 4 cherrystone clams

2 red bell peppers

1 white onion

1 1/2 pounds red snapper cut into bite-sized pieces (make sure there are no bones)

1 pound jumbo shrimp

Pinch of Himalayan pink salt and black pepper

3 1/2 cups seafood broth

1 cup dry white wine

1 teaspoon saffron threads

2 tablespoons minced parsley

8 cloves minced garlic

1/4 cup extra-virgin olive oil, divided

1 large tomato, chopped

2 cups paella rice

4 lobster tails

Lemon wedges, for serving

6 scallions

1 tablespoon freshly squeezed lemon juice

2 teaspoons sweet smoked paprika

INSTRUCTIONS

1 Rinse the mussels and clams and scrub the shells with a brush. Pull out and discard any strings from the shells. Soak the mussels and clams in a large pot of cold water. I do this about 2 hours before cooking, and I change the water a few times. If the clams or mussels open during this time, they are not good, so discard them.

2 Dice the red pepper, scallions, and onion and transfer them, being careful to keep them all separate, to small bowls.

3 Rinse the snapper pieces and transfer them to a paper towel–lined plate. Clean the shrimp, leaving the tip of the tail on, and transfer them to a paper towel–lined plate as well. Leaving the tail on prevents the shrimp from curling up and looks nicer. Season the fish and shrimp with salt and set aside.

4 Heat the seafood broth, wine, and saffron in a large stock pot and keep warm on low.

5 In a small bowl, mash the parsley, garlic, and 1/8 teaspoon of salt together until it becomes a paste.

6 Heat 6 tablespoons of the olive oil in a 15-inch-diameter paella pan or flat skillet over high heat. Place the red snapper into the skillet and quickly brown it, 1 minute on each side. Remove the fish from the pan and set aside.

(continued on next page)

INSTRUCTIONS (cont.)

7   Lower the flame to medium heat and add the peppers first, followed by onions and scallions. Cook both until they are a bit soft. Raise the heat to high again and add the chopped tomato. Stir occasionally for 3 to 5 minutes. It should be starting to look like a sauce.

8   Pour in the broth mix and sprinkle the rice evenly across the pan. Boil for 3 minutes, stirring in the parsley-garlic paste. Add the red snapper back to the pan. Do a taste test to make sure there is enough salt at this point.

9   Lower the heat and allow everything to simmer until it is no longer soupy, but there is enough liquid to continue cooking the rice for 10 minutes. DO NOT stir. You want the rice to get crispy on the bottom.

10   Next, nestle the shrimp, clams, and mussels into the rice so the shell openings face up. Add the lobster tails flesh up. Cook uncovered for 15 to 20 minutes until the rice is almost done. Flip the shrimp as they start to turn pink.

11   Remove the pan from the heat, cover it with aluminum foil, and let rest for at least 10 minutes. Serve portions using a large metal spoon and garnish them with lemon wedges.

THANKSGIVING

Thanksgiving is one of my favorite holidays, not because of the meal, but rather the opportunity to shine a bright and loving spotlight on gratitude. I make many of the recipes throughout this book for Thanksgiving on any given year. There are two things, however, that are must-haves for me on Thanksgiving. One is edible—Apple Crumb Pie—and the other is a "thanking tree."

When our children were small, I'd take a large piece of brown paper, draw a tree, and write: "I am grateful for family, friends, and . . ." The kids would then make construction-paper leaves on which our visitors could write what they were grateful for. It became a beloved family tradition, and it was always a lot of fun reading the responses. My all-time favorite might be my brother-in-law Robert's: "yoga pants." Three years ago, my niece Katey took the reins of this tradition and made a beautiful new style of "thanking tree." You can work out your own plan for the tree. In the meantime, here's the recipe for the pie.

Apple Crumb Pie

Serves 8

Prep Time: 20 minutes · Cook Time: 50 minutes

Tips to make it great:

Use a few different kinds of apples, such as Granny Smith, Gala, or Golden Delicious.

Get someone to help you mix the crumbs. It's more fun that way.

Serve the pie warm with scoops of vanilla ice cream.

For the crust

As I shared earlier, I use frozen pie crust and focus on making the filling and crumbs.

1 9-inch frozen pie shell

Pie Filling

INGREDIENTS

1/2 cup granulated sugar

1/4 cup all-purpose flour

1/2 teaspoon nutmeg

1/2 teaspoon cinnamon

Pinch of Himalayan pink salt

6 apples, peeled and sliced thin
 (about 6 cups of slices)

INSTRUCTIONS

1   Preheat the oven to 425 degrees F.

2   Mix the sugar, flour, nutmeg, cinnamon, and salt in a bowl. Stir in the apple slices. Once fully mixed, set aside.

Crumb Topping

(As noted in my lemon pie recipe, this is the tedious part!)

INGREDIENTS

1/2 cup packed brown sugar

1 cup all-purpose flour

1/2 cup butter at room temperature

Pinch of salt

INSTRUCTIONS

1   Put the brown sugar, flour, butter, and baking powder in a large mixing bowl and with a fork and/or spoon (I alternate between both throughout), begin stirring them together, breaking the butter up and blending it in, until crumbs form. This can take up to 10 minutes of mixing, but stick with it. Once you have fine crumbs, set them aside.

To Assemble

1   Pour the filling into the pie shell and sprinkle the crumbs evenly over the top.

2   Bake for 40 minutes, then cover the pie top with aluminum foil and bake for 10 more minutes, for a total baking time of 50 minutes. Let the pie rest for about 1 hour. Serve each warm slice with a scoop of vanilla ice cream.

CHRISTMAS EVE

All holiday meals reinforce the power of teamwork. As you well know by now, I am blessed with an amazing family I love hosting at my home for the holidays. Teamwork is evident in each and every course; the adage "Many hands make light work" comes to life. I am also fortunate that my cousins often take over cleanup, making sure that every dish and platter is clean before they leave.

On Christmas Eve, we follow the Southern Italian tradition of serving seven (or more!) fish dishes. In addition to the recipes below, our holiday table often includes recipes featured in previous chapters of this book: Shrimp Cocktail (page 8); Scungilli Salad (page 76); Grilled Octopus (page 133); Zuppa di Pesce (page 77); Fried Grey Sole (page 80); and Red Snapper Livornese (page 66).

Holiday Spritz

Makes 1 cocktail

Prep Time: 5 Minutes

When I was dining out in Lucerne, Switzerland, I was curious about the orange-colored drink the people at the next table were having. I tried my first Aperol Spritz on that trip, and I truly can't count how many I've enjoyed ever since! For this Holiday Spritz, I add lime. It's a simple recipe that can put even the grumpiest person into a good mood.

Tips to make it great:

Use a large, festive glass.

Make sure all the ingredients are very cold.

(continued on next page)

INGREDIENTS

4 ice cubes, or as many as desired

2 ounces Aperol

4 ounces Prosecco

Splash of carbonated water or club soda

1 orange slice, for garnish

1 lime slice, for garnish

INSTRUCTIONS

1   Fill a 16-ounce mason jar with ice cubes. Pour in the Aperol, Prosecco, and carbonated water.

2   Garnish with an orange slice and lime slice.

Baked Clams

Serves 4

Prep Time: 15 Minutes

Cook Time: 8 minutes

We always make Baked Clams on Christmas Eve as one of the traditional Italian seven fish dishes. I like littlenecks, and I keep them whole. They are so delicious that I'm not sure why we only make them once a year. I need to change that!

Tips to make it great:

Source littleneck clams.

Don't chop them.

Use extra lemon and oil.

INGREDIENTS

1 dozen clams

1 1/2 cups seasoned breadcrumbs

1/4 teaspoon Himalayan pink salt

1/4 teaspoon black pepper

1 teaspoon grated Parmigiano-Reggiano

1 teaspoon Garlic Paste (see page 17) **or 1 garlic clove, chopped**

1/2 cup clam juice

2 lemons, divided

1/4 cup extra-virgin olive oil

1 sprig fresh parsley, chopped

INSTRUCTIONS

1   Preheat the oven to 400 degrees F.

2   Wash the clams with a brush. Put the unopened clams in a frying pan with a small amount of water at the bottom. Cover the frying pan and heat it over high heat until the clams open.

3   Once the clams have opened, separate the bottom shell (with the clam in it) from the top and discard the top shell. Rinse the clam in the shell. Transfer each shell with the clam in it onto a baking sheet.

4   Mix the breadcrumbs, salt, pepper, cheese, garlic, and clam juice in a bowl. Squeeze one full lemon into the mix. The mix should feel a bit like wet sand.

5   Using a spoon, cover each clam with a healthy portion of the breadcrumb mix. Drizzle the top of each clam with olive oil and bake for around 8 minutes. If you have a broiler, turn it on for the last 2 minutes of cooking. They should be a bit golden and crispy when done.

6   Scoop up any juice in the pan and pour it over the clams. Sprinkle chopped parsley on top of each one and then squeeze them with remaining lemon juice (of 1 full lemon) just before serving.

Squid-Ink Pasta

Serves 4 to 6 (makes 1 1/2 pounds pasta)

Prep Time: 20 minutes

When I was traveling in Italy, squid-ink pasta was served at most restaurants, especially in Venice. The dish looks so striking with its black noodles, and the flavors all combined are nothing short of amazing. Take a risk and try this black-as-night pasta. Word to the wise: in this case, it likely won't work if you tell people it's chicken.

Tips to make it great:

Before you do anything, be sure you've sourced the squid ink.

The more squid ink you add, the darker and saltier your pasta will be.

Have patience and enjoy the process.

Clean your countertop really well.

INGREDIENTS

3 cups all-purpose flour, plus more for dusting

4 extra large eggs

3 to 4 tablespoons squid ink

1/4 cup iodized salt for the boiling water

INSTRUCTIONS

1 Pour all of the flour onto your clean, dry countertop. Shape it into a volcano-like mound with a well (like a crater) in the middle.

2 Carefully crack the eggs into a small bowl, making sure that no pieces of shell get in.

3 Pour the eggs into the middle of the flour "volcano," add the squid ink, and with a fork, beat the eggs into the squid ink until they are black and smooth.

4 Slowly push a little bit of the flour into the inked eggs. It's important that the flour you've moved into the eggs fully absorbs before you push in more flour. Keep using your fork until you have incorporated all of the flour.

INSTRUCTIONS (cont.)

5   At this point, start kneading the dough. If the dough isn't shaping into a "Play-Doh"–like consistency, add more flour gradually. Once the dough is ready, wrap in plastic and set it aside for 2 hours.

6   Cut the dough into 4 pieces. You will roll out each piece separately. To prevent the dough you aren't using from getting dry or hard, keep it covered with plastic wrap.

7   Cover a rolling pin generously with flour. You will need to keep re-flouring the rolling pin on the countertop to prevent the dough from sticking. Take 1 piece of dough at a time and roll it out as thin as possible. It should be about 24 inches long. Take that long strip of dough and fold it, starting from one end, like an accordion. You should end up with a stack that is about 5 layers thick.

8   Cut the dough into thin strands, slicing across the folds of the dough. I like to make fettuccine-wide strands, but you can cut it thinner for spaghetti if you like. After you have cut the dough, transfer each strand onto a paper towel for about 15 minutes.

9   Repeat this process with the remaining 3 sections of dough.

10 When you are ready to cook the pasta, bring a large pot of water to a boil and add iodized salt. Place pasta in the water and cook for about 5 minutes. Remember that fresh pasta always cooks faster than dried pasta. You can also freeze it at this point, tightly wrapped, for use another time.

11 For another special holiday dish, try it with my Zuppa di Pesce recipe on page 77.

Espresso Zabaglione

Serves 4

Prep Time: 10 minutes • Cook Time: 20 minutes

(10 minutes for espresso coffee and 10 minutes for the zabaglione)

For years, my mother-in-law and her sisters always ordered this for dessert when we were out to dinner. And when they did, they'd also always comment on how it was never as delicious as their mom's. While the recipe below isn't either, I can say that it's a very close second.

Tips to make it great:

> Use Ravida Aceto di Vino Marsala wine and Lavazza or Illy coffee.
>
> Serve with fresh strawberries and blueberries.
>
> Serve with biscotti on the side.

INGREDIENTS

1/2 cup chilled espresso coffee

1/4 cup Marsala wine

1/2 cup sugar

6 extra large egg yolks

8 ounces heavy cream

Blueberries and strawberries, for topping

INSTRUCTIONS

1. Make the espresso coffee, set aside to cool, and then refrigerate and chill.

2. Put a bowl in the refrigerator. You will use it to chill the zabaglione when it's done.

3. Use a double boiler or create a makeshift one by placing a heat-proof bowl over a pot of water (enough to sit beneath the bowl when it's placed on top of the pot). Remove the top of the double boiler (or the heat-proof bowl) and bring water in the bottom to a boil over high heat.

INSTRUCTIONS (cont.)

4   In the top of the double boiler (or heat-proof bowl), mix the Marsala wine, sugar, espresso, and egg yolks together until well blended.

5   Place the top of the double boiler (or the heat-proof bowl) over the boiling water and whisk for 4 to 5 minutes. The mixture should become frothy and textured. Remove it from the double boiler and set aside. Once the mixture you prepared is cool, transfer to the chilled bowl, cover, and refrigerate for 2 hours or more before serving.

6   In a medium bowl, whip the heavy cream until it is quite firm. Use this as a garnish on top of the zabaglione, along with a mix of blueberries and strawberries, if you like. If you are feeling fancy, you can prepare small cups with the fruit on the bottom, cover with zabaglione, and top with whipped cream. If you are hosting people who don't like fruit, you can serve the berries and whipping cream on the side.

CHRISTMAS DAY

Some of my mainstay Christmas Day recipes—Spaghetti Primavera (page 88), Sunday Gravy (page 60), Filet Mignon (page 105)—are included in other chapters, but here you'll find my Veal Osso Buco and a few other tried-and-true Christmas favorites.

Brandy Alexander

Makes 1 cocktail

Prep Time: 5 Minutes

This drink was a favorite of my Grandma Millie's, so we naturally learned to make it for her. It's delicious, but she was the only person I knew who could handle more than one.

Tips to make it great:

Serve in a chilled martini glass.

When shaken really well, it turns into a sort of boozy milkshake.

INGREDIENTS

1 1/2 ounces **Remy Martin cognac**

1 ounce **DeKuyper crème de cacao dark liqueur**

1 ounce **heavy cream**

1 teaspoon **freshly grated nutmeg** (you can use pre-ground nutmeg if needed)

INSTRUCTIONS

1 Pour the cognac, crème de cacao, and cream into a shaker filled with ice. Shake until well chilled and the consistency is like a milkshake.

2 Strain into a chilled martini glass and finish it with freshly grated nutmeg.

Lollipop Lamb Chops

Serves 4 to 6

Prep Time: 5 minutes

Cook Time: 10 minutes

Baby lamb chops are a fantastic appetizer. They're also quite easy to prepare on the barbeque or in a grill pan on the stove.

Tips to make it great:

> Ask a butcher to cut the lamb into thin, bite-sized chops.
>
> Do not overcook. Lamb cooks really quickly and continues to cook after you take it off the heat.
>
> Season the lamb chops generously and squeeze lemon on top when they are done.

INGREDIENTS

12 lollipop-trimmed lamb chops

3 tablespoons extra-virgin olive oil

Himalayan pink salt, to season

Black pepper, to season

Garlic powder, to season

Half lemon, for finishing

INSTRUCTIONS

1 Wash the chops and pat them dry. Brush the chops with the olive oil and season them with salt, pepper, and garlic powder.

2 My preferred way to cook these is on the barbeque, even in the winter. Grill them very quickly, 4 to 5 minutes per side. These are best eaten rare. (I have on occasion used a grill pan with excellent results.)

3 Once the lamb chops are cooked and off the grill, squeeze fresh lemon juice over them and enjoy.

Eggplant Rollatini

Serves 8 to 10

Prep Time: 90 minutes (30 minutes active time, plus 1 hour for eggplant to sit in salt)

Cook Time: 60 minutes

The first time I made Eggplant Rollatini without my grandma's support, I thought it would add some "holiday spirit" to use red and green toothpicks, rather than plain ones, to hold the eggplant rolls together. Unfortunately, when I removed the eggplant from the oven, it became apparent that the color of the toothpicks, while harmless, had asserted itself in a colorful way that I hadn't planned, causing more than a few laughs. So, don't do that.

Tips to make it great:

Cut the eggplant as thin as you can for these.

Be very generous with the marinara sauce.

Use wooden toothpicks.

For the eggplant

INGREDIENTS

1 large eggplant

1 tablespoon Himalayan pink salt

5 extra large eggs

1/4 cup whole milk

1 cup all-purpose flour

1 cup seasoned breadcrumbs

4 cups Marinara Sauce (page 190) **or use store-bought, divided**

Extra-virgin olive oil, for frying

INSTRUCTIONS

1   Using a very sharp knife, peel and slice the eggplant into thin, lengthwise slices. An average-sized eggplant should yield about 15 slices, 1/8 inch in width.

2   Salt both sides of each slice, lay a piece of paper towel over each layer of eggplant, and transfer them to a tray. Let the slices sit for 1 hour, or more if you have extra time. This process removes water from the eggplant. Rinse the eggplant lightly and then pat them dry.

3   Beat the eggs in a medium bowl. Add milk and mix well.

INSTRUCTIONS (cont.)

4 Combine the flour and the breadcrumbs in a large flat dish or platter.

5 Dip each eggplant slice into the egg mix and then into the flour-breadcrumb mix. Set aside until you are ready to fry.

6 In a large frying pan over medium-high heat, add the olive oil. Be sure the oil is very hot before putting batches of the eggplant slices in. Fry them for about 2 minutes on each side, then place them on a paper towel–lined platter.

7 Set the oven rack in the middle position and preheat the oven to 375 degrees F.

For filling, forming, and baking

INGREDIENTS

1 1/4 pounds ricotta

1/2 cup grated mozzarella

1/4 cup grated Pecorino Romano, plus more for topping

1/4 cup minced parsley

1/2 teaspoon Himalayan pink salt

INSTRUCTIONS

1 Make the cheese filling by combining all the ingredients in a large bowl and stirring well.

2 Cover the bottom of a 10 by 15-inch baking dish (I use glass pans, but a large aluminum pan works, too) with about 3 1/2 cups of the marinara sauce.

3 Take a slice of eggplant, put 2 to 3 tablespoons of the filling about a third of the way onto the slice, and then roll up the eggplant to enclose the filling. Place a toothpick in the middle so that the roll stays together.

4 Place 1 to 2 teaspoons of marinara on top of the roll (remember to be generous with the sauce!) and sprinkle additional grated cheese on top. Repeat until all the slices are rolled.

5 Bake for 20 minutes and serve hot.

Marinara Sauce

Makes 2 cups

Prep Time: 5 minutes • Cook Time: 30 minutes

In a pinch, I use Lidia's Marinara Sauce. Pomi also makes a marinara sauce, but it is very hard to find. If you have just 35 minutes, please make your own! It's worth it.

INGREDIENTS

2 tablespoon extra-virgin olive oil

1 tablespoon Garlic Paste (see page 17)

1 26-ounce box strained Pomi tomatoes

1 teaspoon Himalayan pink salt

1/4 teaspoon black pepper

INSTRUCTIONS

1 Heat the olive oil in a medium saucepan. When the oil is hot, add the garlic paste. Once the garlic paste gets hot, add the tomatoes, salt, and pepper.

2 Bring to a boil for 3 minutes, then reduce the heat and simmer for 30 minutes. Enjoy right away, refrigerate, or freeze.

Veal Osso Buco

Serves 4 to 6

Prep Time: 20 minutes • Cook Time: 2 1/2 hours

In addition to a holiday entrée, this hearty recipe is great on any winter day. It can be served with pasta to create a whole meal or enjoyed with other dishes. As you'll see, the hole in the bone is filled with marrow, so you can use a fish fork to dig it out and enjoy this delicious treat.

Tips to make it great:

Add lemon zest to the finished dish.

Be patient and let it cook.

INGREDIENTS

4 ounces pancetta, diced into 1/4-inch cubes

All-purpose flour, for dusting the meat before browning

3 to 4 pounds veal shank (4 to 6 pieces, each 2- to 3-inches thick)

2 tablespoons Himalayan pink salt

1 tablespoon black pepper

1 medium onion, diced

1/2 cup diced carrot

1/2 cup diced celery

2 tablespoons chopped garlic (about 4 cloves)

1 cup Barolo red wine

1 to 2 cups chicken or veal stock

Lemon zest

INSTRUCTIONS

1 Preheat the oven to 325 degrees F.

2 Use a Dutch oven or a large ovenproof pot with a cover (be mindful and avoid plastic handles!). Heat the pot on the stove over medium heat for about 5 minutes. Once hot, add the pancetta and cook, stirring occasionally. When the pancetta is crispy and most of the fat has rendered, after about 5 minutes, transfer it to a paper towel–lined plate and set aside.

3 If necessary, drain off all but 2 tablespoons of the fat from the pan.

4 Place the flour in a shallow bowl or deep plate.

5 Season the veal shank pieces well with salt and pepper, then dredge them in the flour. Shake off any excess, and add the meat to the hot fat in the pan.

6 Increase the heat to medium-high and cook the shanks on each side until well browned, about 5 minutes per side. Transfer the shanks to a plate and set aside.

7 Add the onions, carrots, and celery to the pot. Cook the onion mixture, stirring frequently, until the onions are translucent (about 5 minutes) and then toss in the garlic.

8 Continue cooking until the vegetables just begin to brown, about 10 minutes.

9 Add the shanks and the pancetta back to the pan. Pour in the wine and then add enough stock to come a little more than halfway up the sides of the shanks.

10 Bring to a simmer. Cover the pan and transfer it to the oven to cook until the meat is tender, about 90 minutes to 2 hours. The veal should be very soft but not totally falling off the bone. Serve on a large platter.

Millie's Mushrooms

Serves 6

Prep Time: 10 minutes • Cook Time: 15 minutes

This is another one of my grandmother's recipes. There is probably no dish that is equally delicious and simple. I've served these as both an appetizer and as a side dish. I love them so much I could eat them every day!

Tips to make it great:

> Buy mushrooms that are about the diameter of a quarter or a little larger. You don't want them to be too small or too big.
>
> Use extra-virgin olive oil.

INGREDIENTS

12 whole mushrooms

1 cup seasoned breadcrumbs

3 tablespoons extra-virgin olive oil, divided

1/4 cup water

INSTRUCTIONS

1   Preheat oven to 375 degrees F.

2   Wash the mushrooms and be sure to remove any brown specks.

3   Gently remove the stems from the mushrooms, save them, and transfer the mushroom tops to a flat baking dish.

4   Dice the mushroom stems and transfer them to a small bowl. Add the breadcrumbs and mix thoroughly. (I use a fork and mash the mushroom stems into the crumbs as best I can.) Add 2 tablespoons of the olive oil and continue mixing.

5   Take each mushroom cap, fill it with the mixture, and return it to the flat baking dish.

6   Put the 1/4 cup of water into a small bowl and add the last tablespoon of olive oil. Stir the oil and water together, though of course they won't fully combine. Using a teaspoon, put a little bit of oil and water onto each mushroom. If you run out of oil and water, make another batch: 1/4 cup water to 1 teaspoon olive oil.

7   Bake for 8 minutes and then check the mushrooms. If they look a little dry, sprinkle more water and oil on them. Bake for an additional 7 minutes and enjoy.

Aunt Pat's Tri-Color Cookies

Makes about 40 cookies

Prep Time: 60 minutes

Bake Time: 15 minutes

Members of my family have fought over these cookies numerous times. My aunt would make a "square for everyone," but my cousins and siblings would always steal one another's squares and actually hide them. No matter which bakery I buy them from, they're never as good as my aunt's, though Patty Pop's in Pelham, New York, is a very close second (maybe it's the name?).

Tips to make it great:

Watch that the cookies don't burn by checking them regularly, starting at the 10-minute point.

Add some Himalayan pink salt to the top of the cookies after you put the chocolate on.

INGREDIENTS

Cooking oil spray, to grease

2 pounds almond paste

6 sticks butter, softened or melted

1 1/2 cups granulated sugar

8 extra large eggs, yolks and whites separated

2 teaspoons almond extract

4 cups all-purpose flour, sifted

1 teaspoon salt (1/2 teaspoon for the dough and 1/2 teaspoon to sprinkle on top after baking)

10+ drops green food coloring

8+ drops red food coloring

2 12-ounce jars apricot preserves

8 milk chocolate squares

INSTRUCTIONS

1   Preheat the oven to 350 degrees F.

2   Cover three 12x17-inch baking sheets with aluminum foil and coat the foil with cooking oil spray.

3   In a large bowl, use a fork to break up the almond paste. Add the butter, sugar, egg yolks, and almond extract. Beat with an electric mixer until light and fluffy, about 5 minutes. Beat in the flour and 1/2 teaspoon of the salt.

4   In a separate bowl, with a clean set of beaters, beat the egg whites until stiff fluffy peaks form. Use a wooden spoon to fold them into the almond paste mixture to create the dough.

5   Remove about 2 cups of dough (or a little more) and spread it evenly into one of the prepared baking sheets. Remove 2 more cups, add green food coloring, and blend it until the color is even and consistent. Spread the green dough onto one of the other baking sheets.

6   Add the red food coloring to the remaining dough, blending until the color is smooth and consistent. Spread the red dough onto the remaining baking sheet. Each dough layer should be about 1/4-inch thick.

7   Bake the layers for 15 minutes or until the edges are golden brown. You must watch them, because if the batter was not spread evenly, they will burn.

8   Let the layers cool.

(continued on next page)

9   In a small pot over medium-low heat, heat the
    preserves. Once warmed, spread half of it
    evenly over the green layer. Place the yellow
    layer on top of green layer. Spread the
    remaining preserves over the yellow layer, and
    then put the pink layer on top. Cover the
    entire thing with plastic wrap and weigh down
    the layers with a cutting board or heavy plate
    on top. Transfer to the refrigerator and
    refrigerate overnight.

10 The next day, melt the chocolate in a double
    boiler. Spread it all evenly to the edges of the
    top pink layer. Allow the chocolate to cool
    and solidify. Sprinkle salt on top and then cut
    the cookies into small squares.

AFTERWORD:

WHAT'S YOUR FOOD STORY?

Early on in the writing of this book, while reflecting on the ties between food and business, I became curious about how food has been influential in corporate leaders' lives and work. I posed that question to some of them, and here are the responses I received from two wonderful friends.

From Mario Gabelli, chairman and chief executive officer of GAMCO Investors, Inc., the firm he founded in 1977.

"We started buying Danone in 2004, so I had visited the company at its Paris headquarters. Its Dannon brand was the first American yogurt company, located in the Bronx, at a time when yogurt was still a novel product. As a Columbia Business School graduate and member of its Board of Overseers, I have stayed close to the school and many of its professors and students. One of the value-investing professors alerted me to an opportunity involving one of his most promising students. Siggi Hilmarsson hailed from Iceland and was disappointed in the high sugar content of yogurt in the United States. He grew up eating skyr, a thick yogurt that is higher in protein and calcium and lower in sugar and fat. Armed with recipes sent from home by his mother, he decided to start his own yogurt company, producing skyr. I was immediately intrigued with this idea, and my positive thoughts were echoed by my wife, a yogurt enthusiast who had been making her own yogurt since the mid-1970s. I decided to invest. I watched the brand grow its distribution exponentially as it entered Whole Foods stores and many other national chains. Investors were well rewarded when this small, private company agreed to be acquired by Lactalis in 2018."

From Steve Sinacore, chairman of Atrevida Partners, LLC, an investment advisory firm specializing in alternative asset management, a firm he co-founded in 2007.

"Throughout my career, I have been focused on 'fixing the problem'—whether it was internally at J.P. Morgan, or externally by getting companies ready for sale, even on the trading desk. In each case, I realized the essential role teamwork plays in success. I learned this lifelong lesson while making cheese ravioli with my grandparents, parents, and four siblings. We formed a team that would regularly make ravioli from scratch. Each member had assigned, well-defined responsibilities and was held accountable for their role and how it affected other members of the team, from rolling out the dough to filling what would become the pillow pasta, to ultimately counting the number of ravioli in each batch. Every member of Team Sinacore understood that each role was essential to preparing a high-quality deliverable. Focusing on the goal also brought us together in ways that allowed us to leave our differences at the door. The ravioli process helped to shape my leadership style, which is inclusive, goal-oriented, sets high expectations, and celebrates every member of my team (often with a large plate of ravioli)."

How about you? Do you have a food story to share, or maybe a recipe? I've created a web form for the readers of this book to log in, tell a food- or drink-related anecdote, and perhaps leave a recipe. Please go to donnarapaccioli.com/share-your-story to participate. Once I receive enough submissions, I will find a way to compile them for everyone!

ACKNOWLEDGMENTS

It has been such a gift to write this book. I appreciate all the related conversations that my friends, family, and work colleagues—even some people I met for the first time—have endured. They all helped me bring my somewhat random thoughts into what I hope is an enjoyable and informative book.

I believe that you become who you are based on the people you interact with, the experiences you have, and the books you read. I have been truly blessed in my life to be well-educated, to have had a rich set of experiences so far, and to be loved—and in turn to love so many, and still counting.

The most influential people in my life were not well-educated. My grandmother left school before she finished eighth grade to work in a factory to help support her family. Neither of my parents went to college. But all three drove into my soul the importance of faith, education, humility, and empathy. My Catholic elementary school, Sacred Heart Private School, and my high school, Cardinal Spellman, helped to build good habits of inquiry, problem-solving, and discipline. My Jesuit education at Fordham taught me to look for God in all things and gave me the insight to connect seemingly disparate concepts (such as accounting and cooking) and experiences.

I learned from family members and friends who are amazing examples of how to show love, listen to learn, and have fun. While serving as dean of the business school at Fordham, in addition to working with an exceptional team, I traveled to nearly 100 different cities and worked collaboratively with people from Asia, Africa, North America, Europe, and Australia—all of whom shaped my perspectives, and therefore, this book.

As summer 2023 came to a close, along with this book-writing process, the privilege I was most grateful for was being grandmother to Emmy, Chloe, Charlie, and James. Every day, I try to make sure they know they are loved and teach them how to show love for others.

I need to thank a number of people by name for their direct and indirect help with this manuscript. The first is Nicole Gesualdo, who helped me through every aspect of writing this book. Whenever I was frustrated with the way things were turning out (a few publishers turned me down), or had the slightest urge to give up, she would suggest some new way to think about how important and doable the project was.

I am grateful to my husband for reminding me that I was writing the book for myself and our family. Special thanks to my three children and their spouses: Diana and Craig, James and Jackie, and Danielle (also known as my co-editor) and Andrew. Each of you made this book better, and I will always be grateful that you are my family.

I want to thank my mother, Maria, and my father, Richie, who provided me with everything I needed to build a meaningful life, including wonderful recipes (mom) and hysterical stories (dad). My brothers, Anthony and Richie; their wives, Koren and Lisa; and their children have been regular tasters at my table and, more importantly, always there to help in difficult times and celebrate in happy times. My Aunt Pat and her children have been a big part of my life too, and I smile when I think of all the loud meals we have shared and will share in the future.

I have been equally blessed with an amazing group of in-laws. My mother-in-law, Angie, always made cooking and babysitting look easy. When I was a young parent, she and my father-in-law, Frank, would watch our three children so my husband and I could enjoy a night out once a month (sometimes more). Often, she would have three or four of her other grandchildren at her house at the same time. There was always plenty of home-cooked food to be taken home when we picked the children up. I still wonder how she was able to do all of that.

My husband has two brothers, Frankie and Robert, and two sisters, Denise and Maria, who, along with their respective spouses—Mia, Denise, Rocco, and Joe—made me feel like I hit the family lottery. They are fun-loving, there when you need them, and glad to spend time around the table enjoying a cocktail and a meal, and then a second meal, and sometimes a third meal—all on the same day. My nieces and nephews also bring lots of joy to my table.

I want to give a few friends a special thank you. Geri Jansen Klecan, who has been my friend since our first year of high school when she forced (invited) me to skip lunch and go to the social studies resource center, is a source of strength and an example of what hard work, intelligence, and prayer can accomplish. During the most intense point of my career, she gave me a "NO button," which I kept on my desk to counter my tendency to take on too much. My friend Donna Liso has taught me that love is truly boundless. She is always there to answer my calls, enjoy a cosmopolitan with me, and listen until I feel better. Judy Savino, you make me laugh and remind me every time we are together of how important it is to have good friends who are easy to spend time with. And Pat David, thank you for leading me to my book production partner, Stacey Aaronson.

To the others who inspired recipes or guided my thinking as I wrote this book—Greer Jason DiBartolo, Mario Gabelli, Regina Pitaro, Steve Sinacore, Manny Chirico, Angelo Santinelli, Angelo Vivolo, Tanya Bastianich Manuali, Liz Crain, Claire Curry, Al Greco, my co-board members at State Street, my many students and colleagues at Fordham—thank you for supporting me and my project!

I look forward to enjoying the cocktails and meals in this book with all of you!

INDEX OF RECIPES

Index

Index

ABOUT THE AUTHOR

Donna Rapaccioli, PhD, began her career in academia in 1987 at Fordham University, while she was still a PhD student at NYU's Stern School of Business. She spent 20 years on Fordham's faculty before serving as the dean of the Gabelli School of Business, where she holds the rank of university professor and teaches accounting. Throughout her time as dean, she embraced applied learning, encouraging her students to take advantage of the business learning lab that is New York City, and instilled the importance of maintaining a global outlook. She also championed interdisciplinary thinking and collaboration, and established strong ties between academia and industry.

Donna has consulted for financial institutions in the New York area and has guest-lectured on accounting, finance, and leadership. She is also an independent director and trustee on the State Street Global Advisors mutual fund board.

A self- and family-taught amateur chef, Donna's love of the culinary arts began at a very young age. Over the years, she has attended and taught cooking classes to feed that passion. As seen from her recipes, Donna's international travels have influenced her relationship with food, and her portfolio of recipes represents cultures around the globe.

No matter what Donna is cooking, rest assured that it will be simmered and steeped in her grandmother's belief in the importance of sourcing quality ingredients and investing time and love in every home-cooked dish.

Donna most enjoys cooking for her husband, three grown children, and their families. She has shared her recipes with faculty, staff, and students at the Gabelli School for well over a decade, and through this cookbook, she is delighted to share them with readers.

ASA DELLA MOZZARELLA

MANHATTAN, NEW YORK • BABY

MOON • THE BRONX, NEW YORK

ANDAZZO'S FISH MARKET

WESTCHESTER, NEW YORK

INCENT'S MEAT MARKET • PATTY

OP'S • WESTHAMPTON NEW YORK

ASTCHESTER FISH MARKET

STANBUL, TURKEY • CHIN CHIN

GIAMBELLI'S AT 50TH • ISCHIA,

TALY • LUCERNE, SWITZERLAND

EIJING, CHINA • SICILY, ITALY

ARCELONA, SPAIN • POSITANO,

TALY • SANTORINI, GREECE